LIKE NORMAL PEOPLE

LIKE
NORMAL
PEOPLE

ROBERT MEYERS

McGRAW-HILL BOOK COMPANY
NEW YORK   ST. LOUIS   SAN FRANCISCO   LONDON
MEXICO   SYDNEY   TORONTO   DÜSSELDORF

Book design by Stanley Drate.

1 2 3 4 5 6 7 8 9 0 D O D O 7 8 3 2 1 0 9 8

Grateful acknowledgment is made to the National Institute on Mental Retardation, Kinsman NIMR Building, New York University Campus, 4700 Keele Street, Downsview, (Toronto), Ontario, Canada M3J 1P3, for permission to quote from *Normalization: The Principle of Normalization in Human Services*, by Wolf Wolfensberger, © 1972 by the National Institute on Mental Retardation; and to Prentice-Hall, Inc., for permission to quote from *The Wild Boy of Aveyron*, by Jean-Marc-Gaspard Itard, translated by George and Muriel Humphrey, © 1962 by Prentice-Hall, Inc.

Library of Congress Cataloging in Publication Data

Meyers, Robert.
   Like normal people.

   1. Mental deficiency—United States—Biography.
2. Meyers, Robert.   I.   Title.
RC570.5.U6M47   362.3'092'6   [B]   78-9347
ISBN 0-07-041761-X

This book is for
Roger and Virginia Meyers
and
Robert T. and Roslyn Meyers—
who shared their lives, and trusted me to tell their story

PREFACE

For many years I have wanted to tell the story of my family's involvement in the field of mental retardation. That opportunity presented itself in early 1977, when my brother, Roger Meyers, and future sister-in-law, Virginia Rae Hensler, began charging ahead with their long-delayed plans to marry. I felt their wedding would be the perfect peg on which to hang the story of what each of them had endured, the triumphs they had carved out for themselves, and the changes that had taken place in the field of mental retardation which had, in part, made their successes possible.

Roger called me one day in the Washington *Post*'s newsroom and started things off by saying, "Because you're my brother and best friend, I'd like to you to be the best man."

I told him I'd be honored.

Several days later, I told him for the first time of my idea: that I would write a series for the paper on him and our family, using them as examples of people who had lived through the last three decades of change in the treatment of mental retardation. Roger, our parents, and Virginia agreed to cooperate. Selling the *Post*'s editors, however, was a more difficult matter.

After an outline of the proposed series had been passed around, there was initial concern at the paper about the propriety of reporters writing about their own families, not to mention the question of whether such reporting would be accurate or complete.

Additionally, there was great concern about the potentially negative impact such exposure would have on the family.

"There are people who like pulling the wings off of flies," managing editor Howard Simons said one day. "Why subject your family to possible harassment and ridicule?"

My answer, which had been somewhat prepared, was this: Retarded individuals, their families, and friends, have long suffered from a lack of accurate information about them, and they have been stigmatized by a wealth of inaccurate and false beliefs. Very little has been written about the subject for a general audience, and I felt this would be a good opportunity to try to give a full view of the field.

Simons finally approved the project, but established some ground rules: real names could be used (as I wanted), but no exact locations could be printed. The principals would all be urged to get unlisted telephone numbers.

The series was printed on August 21, 22, and 23 in 1977, and reprinted in part around the country during the next several months by subscribers to the Los Angeles *Times*—Washington *Post* News Service. Of the more than two hundred letters I received as a result, only two fell into the crackpot category, although those two were frightening.

During my research for this project, dozens of people gave me the benefit of their time, knowledge, and counsel. Chief among these are my brother and sister-in-law, Roger and Virginia Meyers, and my parents, Robert T. and Roslyn Meyers. Each of them had the courage to answer painful and difficult questions, to dredge up memories left buried for years, and to patiently explain to me again and again how they dealt with the phenomenon of mental retardation. Later, each proofread this book and corrected errors. My love and appreciation for their help can never be fully expressed.

Virginia's mother and Virginia's sister, Carol MacIntyre, also shared their knowledge with me. For this I am deeply indebted.

Among the workers in the field of services to retarded persons, on the local, national, and international levels, the help of these persons, in particular, stands out: Niels Erik Bank-Mikkelsen, Elizabeth M. Boggs, James D. Clements,

Gunnar Dybwad, Richard Koch, Carol Knieff, Fred J. Krause, Paul Marchand and his staff, Frank J. Menolascino, Bengt Nirje, Raymond M. Peterson, Robert Plotkin, Eunice Kennedy Shriver, Bill Stein, Edwin A. Svendsen, and Wolf Wolfensberger.

At the *Post*, Benjamin C. Bradlee made the series ultimately possible by hiring me in the fall of 1975. On this project, I was encouraged by many colleagues, among them Howard Simons, Leonard Downie, Fred Barbash, Judy Nicol, and Felicity Barringer. Others who helped with a kind word when difficulties arose included Donald Baker, Elizabeth Becker, B. D. Colen, Lynn Darling, Walter Douglas, Regina Fraind, Janis Johnson, David Maraniss, Eugene L. Meyer, Mike Weisskopf, and Tom Wilkinson. The series was edited by Donnel Nunes, whose brilliant and sensitive handling of the material cannot be praised enough.

When I traveled during research periods for this book, my friend and neighbor, Hilma Lou Ivey, took care of my home and my cat, Thor, relieving me of anxiety. My agent, Arthur Pine, and book editors, Frederic W. Hills and Peggy Tsukahira, also deserve thanks for their help.

Family members and friends combed their memories and scrapbooks for details to contribute, and their help is gratefully recalled. The manuscript was typed by Mary Palmer.

This has been the collaborative effort of many people, and I have tried to tell the story they told me. Any mistakes in this project are mine; the credit belongs to them.

Alexandria, Virginia
February 1978

1

WHAT MENTALLY RETARDED MEANS

Someone being slow, they are way down low,
Some of them might be alone, in darkness.
These are the severely retarded children and adults.
They may not talk. Some have difficulties
   in learning how to walk. Some may not hear.
Some may not see. They do have this fear
   of darkness
It is hard, this disaster is going too far
   For mental
Retardation is a condition, in the brain, or
   a disease,
Which we do not see.

But we the people, can help the Retarded on
   to a
"Brighter World!"
For Retarded people can learn and earn
The facts of life for their lives.
Some may learn faster than the severely retarded
But they are all under retardation. They all need
A special helping hand. You've got to understand.
Won't you help, with your special-guided hand?

                       —ROGER MEYERS

My brother, who has been mentally retarded since birth and who wrote the poem printed above, took a day off from work last summer to marry the girl of his dreams.

The marriage of Roger Drake Meyers and Virginia Rae Hensler, who also has been retarded from the day she was born, was celebrated in the sun-speckled nave of a California church on June 18, 1977, an otherwise unnoted event among the 3,031 marriages recorded in California that day.

The groom, then twenty-nine, and a permanently-employed part-time busboy in a local restaurant, wore a three-piece black suit, a striped tie, and a carnation in his lapel.

The bride, then twenty-six, and about to begin hotel-employment training, wore a floor-length heavy satin white wedding gown, embroidered with flowers, with a three-foot-long train, a shoulder-length veil, and carried a bouquet of daisies and baby's-breath flowers.

Virginia's mother sat in the first pew on the right as we looked down from the altar, surrounded by her other children, and her grandchildren. Virginia's parents had been divorced many years ago, and her father did not attend the wedding.

Our parents, Robert T. and Roslyn W. Meyers, sat in the front pew on the left side as we faced them, my father wielding a home-movie camera to record the event (it jammed in the middle of the first roll, but he got enough, anyway).

Behind them sat friends, cousins, aunts, uncle, former roommates, schoolmates, and community friends, whom Roger and Virginia had met in their travels through life. ("I'm the bus driver," one man said afterward, meaning that Roger and Virginia used to take his bus as they moved around the community.)

At 1:40 P.M., Sally Weiss, the church organist, who donated her services, sat in the back of the small stucco church playing Mendelssohn's wedding music, while the groom's party solemnly entered along the right-hand aisle. The group was led by Lutheran pastor Edwin A. Svendsen, followed by the groom, then the best man (me), and two young altar boys.

The father of a mildly retarded son who now lives in a group home near his parents, Svendsen had known Virginia for ten years and Roger for seven, having served as the chaplain in the residential facility for the retarded where they had met. He had watched them grow, watched their relationship change from friendship to a brother-and-sister relationship, and then into the love of husband and wife. He had helped guide them through fights, arguments, and employment and sex counseling, and now he was shepherding them through the gates of marriage. They were his children, too.

We took long, slow hesitation steps, eyes always forward, trying to be mature and controlled and not laugh or crack a smile to relieve the pressure. Roger was ramrod straight, his arms at his side, and his eyes glued to the flow of Pastor Ed's white surplice. I was so knotted by anxiety that it was all I could do to follow my brother.

Somehow we made it to the altar, which was decorated with Boston ferns, *Ficus benjamina,* and other plants from a nearby greenhouse, and stopped in front of the stained-glass windows in which an array of symbols—a cross, a star of David, a dove, and a peace symbol—had been scattered like stardust. We turned to face the congregation.

As we did, a little boy holding a white satin pillow in front of him came down the center aisle. On it, tied with yellow satin ribbons, were two wedding rings. Roger and Virginia had paid for them at the local jewelry store at the rate of twenty dollars a week.

Two flower girls came next. They wore filmy dresses and serious faces and strewed rose petals from wicker baskets ahead of the bride.

Then Ms. Weiss hit the strains of what is popularly recognized as "Here Comes the Bride," and Virginia Rae Hensler slowly walked down the aisle on the arm of her older brother. She sailed through a sunshower of flashing lightbulbs and clicking Instamatics, looking beautiful as she floated toward us with a slow hesitation step that accentuated the eternal quality of the moment.

After those seconds that seemed to last forever, she was at the bottom step to the altar, looking up at her groom, fiance, and friend with the biggest brown eyes in the world, being symbolically "handed over" from the arm of her brother and family to the arm of her husband-to-be. Roger took two steps down to offer his extended left arm, and the two of them came back up together.

"Dearly beloved, we are gathered together . . ." Pastor Ed

began, and the miracle was that we were all gathered together—family and friends, retarded and nonretarded—to see a couple celebrate their wedding. Roger and Virginia were about to be wed to each other, but, also, symbolically and emotionally, to be wed to the larger society around them.

A generation ago this marriage probably would not have taken place at all; had Roger and Virginia somehow managed to develop the skills they have so painfully and recently mastered, restrictive laws prohibiting marriage between retarded citizens would have stood in their way.

But a generation ago, they probably would not have been encouraged to develop those skills which compensate for the brain damage that has handicapped each of them. They would have been warehoused, probably involuntarily sterilized, drugged for easy institutional care, and given little more to do than wait for sleep to relieve them of consciousness.

If they had not been warehoused, they would have been ignored, scorned, and ridiculed until they found some small out-of-the-way niche for themselves in a society that then— both in this country and abroad—either irrationally feared them or really didn't give a damn.

The success of Roger and Virginia Meyers, their growing independence, their marriage, and their life together, is the result of their own stubborn intention to free themselves of the shackles of labels, babying, social and parental mothering, and to wrap around them the mantle of normal life that except for "special people" is always taken for granted.

Their intitial success is also due to the sweeping changes that have occurred in the field of mental retardation and civil rights during the generation of their lives. Those changes include not only money spent for the first time on research, facilities, training programs, and counselors, but also a fundamental change in the way the retarded are perceived by themselves and others.

Although many of the awful stigmas and prejudices against the retarded remain, enough headway has been made so that Roger and Virginia and millions of other retarded people like them can now see themselves, and be seen by others, as people who can and should lead productive lives.

Wisdom springs full-blown only from the brow of Zeus; the rest of us have to work at it a bit harder. Much of what I have learned about my brother, my family, myself, and the field of retardation in general was learned because I decided to write about my brother's wedding for the Washington *Post*. My life with my brother was most intense during the years when we were growing up and living with our parents, but that ended a decade ago. My own exposure to Roger's new life as an almost self-sufficient young man was really just beginning. . . .

Late one afternoon, three days before the wedding, I drove Roger and Virginia downtown to the county courthouse to get their marriage license. With us in the rented Chevy Nova was Carol Knieff, their counselor. Her full title is "Follow-up Counselor," and she meets with them for several hours each week to follow up on their semi-independent lives, dealing with whatever problems may arise.

Carol is in her twenties, she has long brown hair, and is one of hundreds of young people around the country who work in the human-services field helping to improve life for the retarded. Her job did not exist a dozen years ago. Quietly and with infinite patience, she listens to Roger and Virginia talk, and struggles with them as they attempt to express their thoughts. Carol makes suggestions on everything from menu planning to appropriate clothing for different occasions, and, in subtle ways, she helps them steer themselves to a more normal life. She works with several other retarded adults in a similar fashion.

"I couldn't do it without their help. I make suggestions, but the interest has got to be there first," she says.

We parked the car about a block from the courthouse.

Once out of the car, Roger and Virginia took off on their own, assuming (as I did) that the courthouse was the largest structure in sight. As we approached the front entrance, Carol said very simply and quietly to them, "Watch for the signs and read them carefully." It was almost a subliminal message, sent up from the unconscious, advice as much as it was reassurance that she would be around if they needed help, but that the primary effort must be their own.

Holding hands, Virginia, with the strap of her white purse draped over her arm, and Roger, slowing his pace so as not to outdistance Virginia who limps (a legacy of the forceps accident at birth, which caused her retardation), went through the oversized doors and then started peering up and around, like travelers reading signs at a foreign railroad station.

The one they were looking for was on their left: MARRIAGE LICENSES. Altering course slightly, they went in. Carol and I followed discreetly behind.

The first counter inside the room had another overhead sign which read: MARRIAGE LICENSE APPLICATIONS. FILL OUT FORMS HERE. They went up to the counter and picked up the stubby yellow pencils. Virginia stayed on the right side and Roger on the left, because she writes with her right hand and he with his left; they know enough about each other to avoid knocking elbows. Carol and I sat on a bench along the far wall.

They took some time filling out the forms. One of the most common aspects of mental retardation is that the ability to think abstractly is lessened. Thinking on their feet is a chore for the retarded. They must mentally fight their way through every situation. The energy they spend on thinking could probably launch a moon shot.

At the same time, people with multiple handicaps, such as Roger and Virginia, must also put enormous energy into such simple tasks as writing. Because of the motor co-ordination problems each has, holding a pencil and writing legibly is another task that requires tremendous concentration. But such tasks can be mastered.

When Virginia and Roger finished filling in the form, they gave the high sign to the clerk behind the counter. Estela M. Rudolph, a woman with gray hair pulled tightly back in a bun, has handled so many of these marriage applications that one seemed no different from another. She joked with the young couple in front of her, but they were too nervous to laugh in return. Ms. Rudolph told them to have a seat,

"The fee is six dollars," she said, swiveling around in her chair.

Virginia reached into her handbag and pulled out six crumpled one-dollar bills. "I've been holding it for weeks." She giggled, waving the money like a torch of freedom.

Twelve states prohibit marriage between retarded persons, according to a 1975 report by the President's Committee on Mental Retardation. As recently as 1971, marriage between retarded adults was prohibited in twenty-four states, or nearly one-half of the states in this country. Roger and Virginia could not have gotten married in her home state of Indiana in 1971, for example, without breaking the law. The restrictive statutes do not say retarded adults; they prohibit marriage between "idiots," "imbeciles," "morons," "the feeble-minded," "the criminally insane," and other such labels which have traditionally been pasted by some people onto others.

Such laws are by-products of the completely unfounded "eugenic scare" and "social menace" crazes of the late nineteenth and early twentieth centuries, but their legacies are still with us today.

"Best of luck," Estela M. Rudolph told them, as she called for the next couple. As Roger's best man (my first such experience, for which I decided to act as his major-domo), I took the marriage certificate from him and we drove home.

"It's amazing how much they can do," Carol Knieff told me later. "But it's amazing, really, only because no one's ever asked them to do anything before. All they need is some help, some guidance, and some encouragement."

Carol's salary is paid by the nonprofit facility in California, where they once lived, which is reimbursed by the state. Roger and Virginia are clients of the facility, which also serves as a disbursement center for services such as hers. She will counsel them at least once a week as long as they qualify for counseling under the federally-established guidelines that are part of the Supplemental Security Income (SSI) Act. Once either Virginia or Roger is off SSI—which may happen for a variety of reasons, including an earned income in excess of roughly $2,400 a year—her counseling will cease.

The next day, my mother and Virginia's mother went to their children's apartments (out of 215 apartments in the complex, five are rented to retarded adults), to prepare for the post-honeymoon shift of Virginia, from the apartment she shared with a roommate, to the two-bedroom apartment she would share with her husband. Roger has always been a compulsive collector and holder of the treasures in his life. Volumes of children's schoolbooks (most purchased since he finished his formal education, with the idea of helping him read and write better), volumes of his poetry (and volumes of copies of his poetry), clothes, dolls, teen-age rock 'n' roll magazines, odds and ends picked up along the way—all this had to be rearranged, taken back with them, or discarded (if Roger could be convinced to give his permission, which he did just as frequently as he withheld it).

As part of his own socialization into the world of marriage, Roger had to be persuaded by his mother to give up some closet space to his bride. His original idea was to clear out two shelves for her, and leave it at that. Since abstract reasoning, or thinking ahead, is difficult, Roger was acting on his own experience, a guideline he uses to judge many things. His own experience did not include sharing an apartment with a wife, so he had difficulty predicting what her needs would be. Once he knew, they split the closet space.

The night before the wedding, Roger and I had dinner with our parents, and, after dinner, I drove my brother home. We talked of many things, including the wedding, their honeymoon, and the new life he was facing. It was a good talk, with a real interplay of emotions and concerns. It was the first of those we have started to have together. At the door to his apartment I said good-night, started to leave, then turned around and hugged him.

The next morning, dressed and shaved, with the wedding

rings in my pocket and the wedding certificate in my hand, I picked up Roger and we started for the church. That's when he informed me he had to go to the bank to get spending money for the honeymoon, and also to pick up some stuffed toy animals, which he had been paying off at the rate of several dollars a week as a kind of informal wedding gift for Virginia.

I panicked. Didn't he realize what time it was? (It was noon, the wedding was supposed to start at 1:30, and the church was ten minutes away. I didn't want to take any chances.) How could he be so calm? He shrugged.

To eliminate the bank run, I gave him twenty dollars, then we hustled through the Saturday morning crowds at the local shopping center—one of the social centers of Virginia's and Roger's lives—to get to the toy store. Roger wanted to chat with the clerks at the counter (he knew them all by name), but I kept insisting that we did not have the time.

"Uh, he's getting married today," I told the clerk in what I hoped was a calm voice. "We're in kind of a rush."

"Oh." She went to the back room, got the stuffed animals (two Dalmatian dogs). We paid the balance due and we were off; Roger carrying the package under his arm.

At the church, Pastor Ed put us in his office, telling Roger to stay there because he was not supposed to see the bride until she appeared at the altar. Roger's friend and former roommate, Alan Lewis, arrived early. Alan began to function as the lookout man, staying outside the study only to rush in whenever a car drove up to say that Virginia "might" be arriving. After innumerable false alarms, *she* arrived and was ushered into another study on the other side of the church.

It wasn't that Roger was so calm but that he was conserving his energies, saving his emotional strength for the ceremony the way a runner saves his energy for the final moments of his race. This, I have learned, is the way both Roger and Virginia operate in their daily lives.

We sat on folding metal chairs in the study, brothers making small talk, mainly saying nothing. Once I got up to straighten his tie; another time I pulled up the white linen handkerchief in his breast pocket to make it look more dapper. I asked myself if

I was babying him, creating a prize package that would look good to everyone but would really disguise his own personality. Then I remembered that friends at my wedding had looked after me in the same way. Grooms are lucky if they are in one piece and shouldn't have to worry about small details.

Someone came up to me in a panic to say that the flowers had not yet arrived. These included the bouquet, the lapel flowers, and the rose petals. I shrugged. What could I do? My responsibility was the groom, and the wedding rings, and they were all here. Eventually, of course, as they do at all weddings, the flowers arrived, and the panic subsided.

"Getting married is like coming out of retardation," Roger told Pastor Ed as he adjusted his surplice. It was one of those off-the-wall remarks that Roger and Virginia both make and which are not the odds and ends of their thinking but show the degree to which they have thought about their lives.

"I'm worried about being able to take care of Roger for the rest of our lives," Virginia was saying about this time to Larry Armstrong, the photographer who had been assigned by the Washington *Post* to photograph the wedding for the series I would write. As she said it, she checked to make sure that she was wearing something old, something new, something borrowed, and something blue. She was.

The trickle of guests had swollen to a flood. About twenty-five people from the residential facility for the retarded where Roger and Virginia had once lived had come by bus and were signing the guest register. Among them was Lionel, a severely retarded man in his forties who had lived in institutions most of his life. One of Roger's jobs at the facility had been to act as a teacher's aide, and in that capacity he sometimes tried to help Lionel read and write. To help him write better, Roger had held Lionel's hand in his own so they could print the letters of his name. Lionel took a long time to sign the wedding guest book that day, but when he was done he had block-printed his first name across the entire entry line.

"Since marriage is a part of God's order of creation, it is to be honored by his people; so we will consider together the meaning of marriage," Pastor Svendsen said. He read from notes he had typed on paper, and which were placed on top of the pages of an open book. The book's binding was a rich, dark red, and it looked to everyone to be a well-worn leather Bible. Actually it was a bound copy of selected passages from Feodor Dostoevsky's *Brothers Karamazov*, which Svendsen had purchased twenty years earlier in Chicago.

"You are here to declare your devotion to each other and to join yourselves in marriage. The rest of us are here to witness your declarations to each other and to wish you joy in your growing together.

"All of us are aware, as you two are also, that God's spirit is alive among us, prompting, listening, and encouraging! He has found us long before we ever sought Him, and He is here in Spirit and through His Word.

"The church has spoken through the Word, saying, 'God created us in His own image, and He created us male and female.' The celebration of marriage is for the joy of living together and belonging to each other," Svendsen told them and the congregation. "It is God's will that you will live together in His world, related in love to each other. He will bless you and also charge you with responsibility toward each other and toward all people. . . ."

"Tell them that getting married is like coming out of retardation," Roger unexpectedly cued him, *sotto voce,* echoing a theme that for years had been one of his hallmarks. Startled, Svendsen decided to go along with the suggestion.

"Roger wants me to remind you that getting married is like coming out of retardation and into the larger community," Svendsen said, incorporating Roger's point into his theme, but trying to keep track of his own thoughts. (In his thirty-three years as an ordained minister, it was the first time that any groom had ever helped him with his remarks. ". . . and I appreciated it," Pastor Svendsen said, later.)

"And say that we met at the bunny rabbit," Roger cued him again, *sotto voce,* his right hand gesturing slightly for emphasis, his voice so low that no one in the front pews could hear him. The bunny rabbit had been on display at an arts and crafts exhibit at Roger's and Virginia's residential facility.

"And that they met at the bunny rabbit, which reminds us that in Matthew we read of the words of Jesus that you two shall become one flesh in beautiful ways of loving and caring. As this happens, the father and mother ties will pale as you grow in strength and oneness, because God has joined you together, and no one will separate you."

These last comments had been carefully worked out among the bride and groom and minister. There had been people who had been opposed to the marriage, or who worried out loud about whether the young couple could handle the responsibility of it, and handle their obligations to themselves and society at large. Those fears had been conquered, or at least silenced, but not without misgivings and certainly not without a struggle. Nonetheless, they had been overcome. But for the parents on both sides of the aisle, those words meant Virginia and Roger were going on their own.

". . . and say that Virginia has brown eyes, like the bunny rabbit," Roger cued Svendsen again, *sotto voce*, beginning to warm to the task of directing the minister's speech at his own wedding. ". . . and that ever since then I've called her my bunny." The minister declined to be led any further, and decided to finish the remarks he had prepared.

"In this oneness which is God's gift to you, you will cherish each other, delight in each other, accent each other—the attributes of personality each one has, the character and ideals and the imperfections of each other. In this oneness may you never seek to grow apart through indifference, through preoccupation, through lesser concerns. May you always seek to be renewed through God's will and Spirit."

Then Svendsen had the couple, who had been facing him, turn to face each other, and hold hands. The pastor saw Roger's knees begin to shake.

"Roger, do you choose Virginia to be your wife? Will you love, respect, and honor her? Will you share your plans and interests, ideals and emotions, through crises and anxiety, through joy and pleasure, caring for her in lifelong commitment?"

"Yes," said Roger Drake Meyers, biting down hard on the end of the word, because S sounds have always given him trouble.

"Virginia, do you choose Roger to be your husband? Will you love, respect, and honor him? Will you share your plans and interests, ideals and emotions, through crises and anxiety, through joy and pleasure, caring for him in lifelong commitment?"

"Yes," said Virginia Rae Hensler, using a voice whose very modulation and clarity was the result of her effort at overcoming several speech impediments, imposed by the physician's accident at her birth, a voice that as much as anyone's carried an affirmation of life.

"Please repeat after me," Svendsen instructed them, and they followed his orders. Virginia's eyes and Roger's eyes were locked in each other's, just as were their hands. They spoke the phrases in turn as Svendsen said them; Roger first, then Virginia.

"I join you in marriage . . . to know you as my wife . . . to share all of life with you . . . its responsibilities and freedoms . . . its tensions and trials . . . to cherish and care for you . . . and with you to follow God's leadings. . . . This is my promise to you."

When they had finished, Svendsen began again: "You two have shared with each other your open and honest commitment before all of your friends. You can make it new every day as you strive to know one another in the Christian sense of knowing the whole person—body, mind, and spirit. I know you will respect the solitude of each other, the right to be a person without being completely dependent on each other. It was never intended that closeness means domination, or the 'right' to pry. Willingly may you share and grow in the unfolding love of two people with God's spirit within and around you."

The members of the congregation were quite still, watching this ceremony in front of them, the vault of the ceiling high above their heads, a warm glow pervading the sanctuary.

Svendsen turned to the little boy holding the white satin pillow, who had been shifting his weight from one foot to the other, and untied the two yellow ribbons holding the wedding rings. The pastor's hands shook with nervousness and concern.

"Virginia," he said, and Virginia took the gold wedding band from Svendsen, using her right hand (the stronger of her two hands, the left being weaker as a result of the forceps accident at her birth), and started to slip it on the fourth finger of Roger's left hand.

"I give you this ring as a sign of my love and faithfulness," Virginia said, repeating the words after Svendsen. She had to push it a little with her left hand to get it over Roger's knuckle.

"Roger," Svendsen said, handing him the ring with its ten diamond chips and watching as he gingerly held it between his thumb and forefinger and slipped it onto Virginia's finger.

"I give you this ring as a sign of my love and faithfulness," Roger repeated.

Svendsen now put his hands on theirs. "Since you have already declared yourselves in the presence of God to be married, you are now married in the name of the Father and the Son and the Holy Spirit," he said, as a rush of smiles filled the church. "You may kiss the bride."

It was a good long smacker, too, with an embrace and a hug to each other from a couple who had never written themselves off. They had overcome physical and mental handicaps of their own, wild and vicious handicaps on the part of other people toward them, prejudices against people who are supposed to be "different," even though they are more like the rest of us than not. They had overcome ignorance, arrogance, stupidity, and a whole array of wrongs and insults had slowly been changed—though they are not completely gone—in the decades of Virginia's and Roger's lives. They had moved from restrictive institutional environments into supervised apartments and then into apartments of their own in the "regular" community. Now they were about to move in together as a married couple.

They turned to face the congregation, and again that happy hailstorm of popping lightbulbs came tearing at them. Virginia's dress was so heavy and long that there had been concern that while she was descending the stairs the material might catch under her shoe. So her matron of honor and sister-in-law picked up one side of the train and moved it around so that it was squarely behind her, and I knelt down to straighten out the other corner of the train. Then Mr. and Mrs. Roger Drake Meyers walked down the steps and into their new life.

After the wedding there was a reception at a nearby motel, where beribboned gifts were piled high on tables, and the bride and groom were toasted with endless glasses of champagne. After that I drove them to the rambling Victorian-era beach-front hotel where they would spend their honeymoon. As we sped along the freeway, I saw them in the rear-view mirror asleep in each other's arms, their heads resting together, dreaming champagne dreams.

They awoke as we approached the hotel, immediately excited. I unloaded the bags from the car, gave them to the bellman, then stayed out of their way.

It was Virginia who found the registration line, keeping Roger right by her side and telling the clerk that they had a reservation which was a gift from the best man.

After registering, the bellman led them up to their room, explaining the history of the hotel to them as he does with every guest who checks in. I didn't hear the whole speech or see their room because I left.

Later, however, I discovered that they had not at all liked their inside room, because its view looked out only on other buildings. The new Mrs. Meyers had complained in no uncertain terms to the management that a new room, with an ocean view, must be found. And it was.

During their honeymoon, which was traditional in every sense, they walked hand-in-hand along the beach, went to the hotel's sauna lounges for a bath and massage, window-shopped along the sidewalks of the small resort community, ate a pizza for lunch, bought magazines to read, and began living with each other as man and wife.

Virginia's wedding ring felt loose to her ("I was afraid I was going to lose it," she said) so they located a jeweler, and left the ring to be fixed. Then, to make sure they would be able to make it back on their own to pick up the ring in a week's time, they stood outside the shop and waited for the next bus to come by. They memorized its number, and when they came back on that bus the next week, made a day of it by taking along a picnic lunch to eat at the beach.

Such actions—registering at a hotel, complaining about the location of a room, taking a wedding ring to be fixed—are actions that neither would have been able to perform at all or as well several years ago, but which they now can and do perform all the time, as they help and complement each other.

After the two-day honeymoon, the couple returned home to receive friends.

THE SILENCE OF LOVE

You and your friend	went up on a hill
You and your friend	stood very still
And you both listen	to the silence of love

—ROGER MEYERS

The most frequently used definition of mental retardation was adopted in 1973 by the American Association on Mental Deficiency (AAMD), the group representing the professionals in the field. It holds that mental retardation exists when an individual achieves an I.Q. rating of about 70 (or less), when he or she has significant social-adjustment problems, and when these two phenomena appear before the age of eighteen.

Mental retardation affects as many people as blindness, cerebral palsy, and rheumatic heart disease combined; and before the development of the Sabin/Salk vaccine, polio victims could be added to that list. One out of every ten persons in this country is a parent, sibling, or personal friend of a retarded person.

American authorities say that 3 percent of the U.S. population—currently, 6.3 million people—will be regarded as retarded at some time in their lives. At any particular moment, 1 percent of the U.S. population, or 2.1 million people, can be regarded as retarded.

The difference in numbers reflects the fact that it is often difficult to tell whether a person is retarded, and it is unfair to label him as such if he has overcome his handicaps. Most retarded people—75 to 90 percent—are mildly retarded, meaning they are very much like Roger and Virginia. They are able, with help, to function with a high degree of independence and individuality.

The numbers game is always tricky because it is based on a *perception,* which may turn out to be incorrect. A child classed as "moderately" retarded may actually turn out to be "mildly" retarded—or maybe he just did not understand the test. In one study done among Mexican-American children in Riverside, California, nearly 15 percent of them were "found" to be retarded. But as adaptive behavior and culturally adjusted tests were applied, this number was reduced to only 1.53 percent, which is consistent with weighted studies for society as a whole.

With that as a warning, the following table might be found to be of use—but only if taken with one parent's warning that "I've never believed I.Q. tests. I always thought my son had more potential than he was showing." The parent was my father and he was talking about my brother.

LEVEL OF MENTAL RETARDATION	I.Q. RANGE	PERCENT OF RETARDED POPULATION	PERCENT OF NONRETARDED POPULATION
Mild	50–70	89	2.67
Moderate	30–50	6	0.18
Severe	20–40	3.5	0.105
Profound	0–20	1.5	0.045
		100	3.00

There are now more than 250 identified causes of mental retardation. Roughly 85 percent are nonorganic, which include accidents at birth, undetected trauma, inborn errors of metabolism, poor nutrition, illness during pregnancy, and hundreds of other factors.

Genetic disorders account for approximately 15 percent of the cases, and these are usually associated with the classes of retardation known as moderate, severe, and profound. Still, in three out of four cases of mental retardation no one can say for sure what was the cause. One out of three mentally retarded persons has additional handicaps similar to Roger's, such as speech impediments and faulty motor co-ordination.

Proof that retardation is whatever we say it is and that the retarded are persons we label as such, is this: When Roger was growing up, he was often labeled as "borderline" retarded, since on some tests his I.Q. was placed above 70 (with 100 representing "normal" intelligence). The borderline-retarded category ran from about 70 to about 85. (Between 85 and 100 were persons with "dull-normal" intelligence.)

In 1973, the American Association on Mental Deficiency *abolished* the borderline category of retardation, and so people previously classified as borderline retarded now found themselves classified as people with borderline intelligence.

"They were probably better off," says James Clements, M.D., who became head of AAMD the following year. "That way they don't carry the stigma of being retarded." (Educational and other aid was still available to them, however.)

The Romans abandoned their retarded offspring on hillsides. In the Middle Ages the retarded were forced to become dunces, fools, and, literally, bait in the bear pits. In the Age of Enlightenment in England and France, people paid to see them at "hospitals." In colonial America they were burned at the stake as witches. In more recent times, mental retardation was virtually the only human disability for which incarceration, or institutionalization, was regularly recommended by the medical profession. The retarded were scorned and denied their humanity. Sometimes they have been denied their very lives, for example, in cases where physicians or parents refuse to surgically correct upper-respiratory blockage that is usually associated with Down's Syndrome newborns. The babies then starve to death. According to doctors who are critical of their colleagues, the standard medical reply to a question about Down's Syndrome children was: "Oh, you mean the Mongoloid kids? They have a very short lifespan." With medical attention, of course, that lifespan can be lengthened. In fact, in just the past few years, it has been more than doubled—from about fifteen to about forty years.

In the period immediately after World War II, there were, essentially, three options urged on those millions of American couples whose children would be classed as retarded: warehouse them, keep them at home and out of the way, or place them in expensive private-care facilities. There were some pockets of interest—scattered individuals who sought to fan the spark of life, people who thought retarded children did not have to become diapered adults, and people who did not think the retarded were not automatic criminals and their parents objects of scorn and rejection—but they were few and far between.

The new phenomenon "television" was introduced into carpeted living rooms. A haberdasher from Independence, Missouri, was in the White House. The post-war economy was on the "upswing"; it was a word and an image that once again showed America's confidence in herself and her possibilities. Housing was up, Joe Di Maggio reigned supreme in center field—by God, this was a good country to live in! For the parents of the mentally retarded, however, these were still the "dark ages."

Roger Drake Meyers was born at 11:55 A.M. on August 8, 1948, the second child of Roslyn Willinger Meyers, who was one month shy of twenty-nine, and Robert Townsend Meyers, then thirty-eight. Roger was born at full term, weighing five pounds, and with no complications during the two-minute delivery at Kew Gardens General Hospital in Queens County, New York. The attending physician was a general practitioner and family friend, Joseph G. Blank, M.D.

"I delivered you very quickly," our mother told me, "so when I went into labor with Roger, I told the nurse that I delivered quickly. Dr. Joe wasn't around; he was downstairs getting a pack of cigarettes, and when the labor pains started coming more quickly the nurse told me to cross my legs to delay the birth. Which I did, for a minute or so.

"I've always thought that something happened when I crossed my legs, that Roger's retardation was caused by me . . . there was an oxygen loss, or something happened. I do remember having a cold for a few days during pregnancy; maybe that did it," she said.

Two days before, on August 6, she had gone into a false labor and had been rushed to the hospital. Although she was soon sent home, there had been some spotting on the sheets. This may have meant nothing or it may have indicated an early break in the amniotic sac surrounding the child, which might have indicated a lessening of oxygen to the fetus, a cause of brain damage.

Whatever the cause, a son, who would later be labeled as retarded, had been born. "It became a fact of life, something we lived with. It became natural for us to have one son who is retarded," our father said.

Roslyn Meyers was then a slender woman with olive-toned skin and brunette hair which she kept at shoulder length. The calmness in her face in the pictures of her at that time contrast painfully with the tension and pressure seen in later photographs as her son's retardation became evident.

Bob Meyers was a red-headed businessman, with a heavy chest and spindly legs. He was a man with a temper, who prided himself on keeping his feelings hidden.

After twelve days in the maternity ward, Roger was wrapped in blue family blankets (which once had been wrapped around me) and brought home by his proud parents in a rambling maroon Buick convertible.

Home was a two-bedroom apartment on the third floor of the Georgian House, a six-story red-brick building about a mile from the hospital in Kew Gardens, New York.

Kew Gardens then was much as it is today—a pleasant neighborhood of six-story apartment buildings and single-family homes, maple and elm trees which flower green in spring and die a brilliant yellow death in the fall, and small shops run by Jewish immigrants, or Italians, or Poles. Today some of the new upwardly mobile groups, the Puerto Ricans and Koreans, have moved in as well, following the immigrants' path "up" from Brooklyn and the Bronx.

Queens then represented something called "the country" to that peculiar New York City way of looking at things, and it was to Queens and a ninety-two-dollars-a-month, two-bedroom apartment that my parents moved in 1943. I was born shortly afterward, five years before Roger.

Roger at first stayed in a crib in my parents' room, then moved in with me.

"He was a quiet baby in the daytime, but he cried and cried at night. I nursed him for a month, then he wouldn't take it anymore. Sometimes he'd be bright and active, and then lethargic, his head drooping, and he'd lie there. He looked like the sweetest baby in the world," our mother said.

Because of the inconsistencies in his behavior during the first few months of life and her memories of my comparatively uncomplicated behavior at a similar period, my mother started to be concerned that something was the matter with her second son.

"I'd wake up, in the middle of the night or the early morning, wondering if I'd done something wrong, wondering if there was anything I could do."

Definite suspicions of retardation, frightening for any mother to contemplate, were pushed to the back of her mind until her own mother arrived from California to visit her six-month-old grandchild.

"She thought Rogie was weak. She'd put her hand in front of him and hold out her finger for him to do finger-pulls; he couldn't do them. I didn't know what to say."

With the bustling affection of the all-knowing grandmother, Teresa Lustig Sinai kept pestering her dark-haired daughter for answers, receiving weak assurances in return. But back home in Oakland, Mrs. Sinai let her concern out.

"She said he doesn't hold his head up; it falls back on the pillow. She said he doesn't respond like he's supposed to," my mother's brother, Joseph M. Sinai, recalled. "She said, 'Roz kept saying everything's going to be all right, but I've held too many babies; there's something the matter there.' Then she'd pace back and forth, wringing her hands."

Thus was established, very early on, one of the great themes of difficulty throughout our parents' lives—acknowledging to themselves that something was wrong but denying it to others.

In many ways it is hard to blame them—with no medical specialists to conclusively say Roger was retarded, why take on the burden and stigma if he might not be? But if he was, then he would have to be "warehoused" (the doctors said so), and how could they face that?

To deny it was to fly in the face of observation, and yet that denial is one of the reasons Roger has developed into the person he is: By denying to themselves and others that he was retarded, they unconsciously and indirectly set out to prove he was *not* retarded, and so gave him as many experiences as a non-retarded person would get. That is just what the experts recommend today. My parents' denial created personal confusion and misdirection of purpose, but it also, ironically, helped Roger develop the strong sense of self which carried him through the frustration and mockery that was to come.

"What could we do?" my father asked. "In those days there were no centers that specialized in dealing with this, no place you could go for information. We didn't know what to do, and didn't know how to do it. I, for one, kept thinking, hoping, that he would snap out of it."

"We knew Roger was different, but we didn't know why. No one ever asked your parents directly, 'What's exactly wrong?'" Barbara Felsing de Pasquale, who was then our downstairs neighbor and Roger's teen-age baby-sitter, and is now the mother of three, recalled.

My mother remembered: "I'd put him in the stroller and take him to the park, and he'd laugh and look around or else be very quiet. When we got one of those toddler toys (a contraption in which the child sits in the middle and pedals himself around), he'd go like a son of a gun, but then kind of sink into himself."

Roger was small, with pale, pale skin and fragile bone structure. He sat up at the age of one and at the same age spoke his first words—"Da, Dada," He walked at two, strung words together at three, but by three-and-a-half he was still only repeating sentences rather than initiating them, according to our mother and the medical reports.

He couldn't pronounce words clearly, and for many years I was the family "translator," telling my parents what Roger had said—a common occurrence when one child in the family has a speech problem.

Roger had trouble keeping his balance and fell down often. He could not make his body work as he wanted it: When he was two years old he was hit by a bicycle and fell down on his forehead; his collarbone was twice broken by falls before the age of five. On those occasions he had to wear enormous plaster-of-Paris casts on first one clavicle, then on the other, which made him look like the junior member of the football team.

Often, he was unable to get to sleep. When he did, he slept so soundly that he could not be awakened, which compounded a long-standing problem with bed-wetting. Of the many behavior-modification approaches our parents tried to correct his bed-wetting, one was a commercial device in which a bell was set off at the first contact with wetness. The idea was that the individual would then get up and conduct himself properly. The device worked brilliantly for everyone except Roger.

"We'd tell him time and time again to remember, 'When the bell rings, I will get up. When the bell rings, I will get up.' So every time the bell rang, we all got up; your father and I and you, too, bumping into each other in the hallway and the bedroom, trying to find the light switch, knocking over the lamps, and all the time the bell was ringing Roger was sleeping soundly," our mother recalled, laughing.

Roger was fascinated by anything that moved quickly, from automobile tires on moving cars to the rackety subway cars on the Jamaica Avenue El to spinning pots and pans and flushing toilets. He could watch these things for hours on end, spinning the top when it stopped, reflushing the toilet over and over again, always standing near the object, bending over to watch it more closely, and, in a classic example of self-stimulating behavior, shaking hands with himself.

On September 28, 1950, Roger, dressed in his light brown herringbone topcoat with the velvet collar and a peaked beanie-style cap from Best & Company, was taken into Manhattan for the first of dozens of medical examinations and consultations that he would have before he reached young manhood. Today there are research centers, children's hospitals, university-affiliated clinics, medical specialists in mental retardation, and social- and human-service workers, who deal with "mentally retarded," "developmentally disabled," "disadvantaged" youngsters, or whatever term is in vogue, but in those days there was no one place a parent could go for comprehensive information.

Our family physician had been unable to find a specialist in the field of mental retardation because there was none. On their own, after reading an article he had written in the *Reader's Digest,* our parents found a man whose subspecialty was in the field. But he was no more helpful than anyone else.

The information they got in all those visits was specialized and was never explained to them in terms they could understand. One physician tossed off that Roger "might" achieve a mental age of "Oh, nine or ten," reinforcing the false idea that Roger would always be a child. The doctor neglected to say that the upper mental age limit on I.Q. tests was sixteen, nor did he explain, if he knew it, that people rely far more on their social knowledge rather than on their intellectual knowledge during their lifetimes. None of the specialists ever mentioned the possibility of early intervention programs involving intellectual and motor stimulation. Today, such programs are regarded as crucial to the full development of any individual's potential. In Roger's case, those programs might have been started as early as six months, as soon as he was observed having problems doing finger-pulls with his grandmother.

The first medical report and a subsequent one on April 2, 1951, found Roger had "borderline level of intelligence," with an I.Q. level of 75. Roger was learning, though at a slower rate than other children. Indistinct speech was seen as a cause of difficulties in learning and in socialization. Additionally, "the examiner believes that the mother is too demanding and may be comparing Roger unfavorably with his older brother." That statement did nothing for our mother's self-confidence.

On December 17, 1951, Roger was sent to the Hospital of the Rockefeller Institute in New York because of "mental deficiency and retarded development." This examination showed a bone age of 1.8 years compared with a chronological age of 2.7 years, and a daily one-gram dose of thyroid medication was started.

Another report from the same hospital on June 27, 1952, stated that Roger had grown 1.25 inches in six months and had gained 1.25 pounds. His motor ability and speech were also seen as improving and his fingernails, which for unknown reasons were soft and grew slowly, had shown some improvement.

On December 7, 1953, a psychological consultant wondered whether Roger had a hearing problem which impeded his comprehension. This worker also said that Roger exerted the "maximum effort for a minimal end result," which was a way of saying he was trying too hard!

On May 10, 1954, a physician tested Roger for sensory motor aphasia, and concluded that it probably was not the cause of his difficulties, but suggested, instead, that a "congenital abnormality of the brain hemispheres" was the problem. A pneumoencephalogram, a risky procedure in which fluid is extracted from the brain and replaced by air, oxygen, or helium, which is then photographed by medical X-ray and analyzed, was suggested to and rejected by my father.

On February 26, 1955, Roger was examined by a doctor who specialized in hearing problems. The man concluded that while Roger's hearing was normal, he might have enlarged adenoids which would have contributed to his speech impediment. (One footnote to history: the speech technician was Anna Freud, daughter of Sigmund Freud.)

Although these medical reports state crisply and simply the medical conclusions of the specialists consulted, they do not tell the story of the frustration my parents and brother were going through.

"One of these clowns told us to be happy that Roger lived in the age of electronics, so he could get all his information about the world from television, because he would never learn to read or write," our father says, bitterly.

"Another man told us to 'warehouse' him immediately, that there was no hope for him. Somebody else suggested a new surgical procedure, just going on in Switzerland, which might find out what the problem was—even though the operation had a high fatality factor. Another guy suggested megavitamin therapy," he said. Other physicians, basically, sought to soothe.

"They told us that such and such was the problem, but that

it would go away or that there was nothing really to worry about," said our mother. "But it's so devastating to be told that when you know, you just *know*, that there's something the matter."

Roger tried so hard, dutifully going to every examination, putting up with tests and quizzes and needles that were poked in him; having strange people in white coats ask him questions and then, often, discuss his "problems" in front of him with my parents (which they did not like but never complained about).

Because of his faulty motor co-ordination, one of Roger's favorite activities was sitting and listening to his records, especially one called "The Little Gray Ponies," which he played over and over and over again.

"When he'd try to keep up with the kids in the apartment building he couldn't; he'd get so frustrated he'd either shake his hands, or his face would turn white, or he'd just go back to his room.

"He always had nightmares, and he'd wake up screaming. I've always thought he was trying so hard to keep up, to make his fingers work the way he wanted them to, to make his mind work faster than it was going, that he'd wake up screaming because he was so frustrated, because that was the only way he could express his anger," our mother remembers.

Roger's and my beds stood head to head along the left wall, the furniture a colonial-style maple. When Roger had trouble sleeping at night, I would put my right arm through the headboard and hold his hand, trying to comfort him.

Once I was falling asleep faster than he was but did not want to take away the comfort he got from the contact with me. So I got out of bed and put on one of my winter gloves, climbed back in bed, put my gloved hand through the headboard, and held his hand. A few minutes later, I slipped my hand out of the glove, which he was still clutching. I hoped he would think he was still holding my hand, but I had not fooled him. After he looked at me, I put my hand back in his.

In our family album is a picture of Roger taken some years later when he was six or seven. In the picture he is a skinny kid, with piano legs sticking through khaki shorts, wearing a white

T-shirt. He is fishing with his uncle, Joe Sinai. Roger's tongue is stuck firmly in the corner of his mouth, as he tugs on a fishing pole, on which must be hooked the biggest fish in all America.

Roger has always been like that, even as a kid—stubborn as the morning, not giving in.

The fish got away.

 **3**

TRADING

One boy said, can I have your big giant pencil?
The kid said no.
OK I'll trade you for my toad, it never grows old.
I'll trade you for a big Monopoly game,
For a small one, it goes the same.
I'll trade you for my ball, I know you know it all.
I'll trade you for my train,
It's starting to rain.
So can't I have your giant pencil please? No?
Oh well, skip it. I guess I never win but someday
I will.

—ROGER MEYERS

When we receive something unexpectedly or painfully, it can seem as if this is what we deserve.

That was the emotional dilemma my parents found themselves in as Roger's problems became more apparent and the answers less than satisfactory.

Michael J. Begab, Ph.D., head of the Mental Retardation Research Center's branch of the National Institutes of Health, put it this way: "It's inevitable that a retarded person will have a significant impact on his family. The experience can enrich lives or it can confuse them, but it is too significant an event not to have any impact at all."

"Having a retarded child does not have to be the end of the world, but you've got to be able to handle stress well," said Frank J. Menolascino, M.D., former president (1975 to 1977) of the parent-oriented National Association for Retarded Citizens (NARC). "You've got to have good support systems—brothers, sisters, and cousins you can turn to—and good professional service, which just did not exist then."

There were no local parent groups in our area that my parents knew of at the time Roger was growing. The NARC, which in the 1960s was such a powerful lobbying group for the retarded and their families, was not formed until 1950, when Roger was two, and did not really begin to exert power on behalf of the retarded and their families until a decade later. The federal government did not employ its first full-time specialist in the field until 1956 (Rudolph Hormuth is still on the job at HEW); and local and state support for the retarded and their families was virtually nonexistent—except where expressed in the form of institutions, a specter that haunted my parents' generation.

As Roger listened over and over and over again to "The Little Gray Ponies," or fell down, or cried in frustration, or as physicians in white coats used Latin-edged words to describe medical phenomena that seemingly bore no relation to their son, my parents' habitual method of dealing with life and with stress was called upon and was often found wanting.

"We didn't know where to go or where to turn," my mother said. "We felt, I felt, so lost and alone."

She was born on September 25, 1919, in Oakland, California, the second child of Teresa Lustig and Joseph Willinger. Her mother, a large-boned woman with a booming laugh and a crackling sense of humor, raised her two children by herself after she was abandoned in 1924 by her husband. Teresa Willinger later married Charles Sinai, a dentist, and had another child, Joey, now also a dentist. He is the uncle with whom Roger was photographed fishing.

So as our mother trudged the streets of Manhattan with her infant son, going from doctor's office to laboratory to examination room, trying to find help for Roger and not someone else to tell her that this was "something" he would grow out of, it was easy for her to fall back on the feelings of repudiation and scorn she had herself experienced as a child.

"We'd be walking along, the two of us, and I felt like we were two rejects, him and me. Society had rejected him, and I was rejected myself. We only had each other to share our feelings with," she said.

Once, years later, at the Museum of Modern Art in New York, they saw a Picasso masterwork, *Woman in a Mirror*. It shows a woman, possibly a pregnant woman, whose image is fractured into a thousand planes and shapes. Roger saw it as a metaphor, a visual statement of what he was seeing around him, feeling what his mother next to him felt, which neither of them could articulate.

"Roger was very good in art, and he copied it for me," my mother recalled. He used as his guide a ten-cent postcard which they bought in the museum's gift shop. For years later, this wrinkled, crumbled postcard stayed with him, traveling with him like a testament.

For my father, this period was equally difficult. Though he said little to friends about his concerns for his boy, he raged against the doctors. Why could they tell him nothing of value and little of hope, if American medicine was the finest in the world?

Robert Townsend Meyers (the middle name was not given at birth but adopted in his twenties) was the second child of Clare Ehlin and Frank Meyers. Clare was a registered pharmacist who once owned her own drugstore on Lexington Avenue, and Frank was a night-school lawyer who had gone into the magazine business. Dad had worked since the age of twenty, and later supported his parents for many years. Neighbors often turned to him for financial advice, even though some of them were better off than he was.

Our father's early work was in the proprietary drug field, first as a salesman, with a dozen eastern states as his territory, then as a national sales manager, flying around the country to check on clients. A genuine whiz kid, he had his picture on the cover of a national trade magazine when he was only twenty-five. In later years, he moved from merchandising into advertising, still dealing with over-the-counter products, such as cold remedies and facial preparations.

As Roger's situation became clear, our father began to believe that the answer lay not in the medical field, which only bled him of money and strength, but in some kind of a "financial killing," which would enable him to guarantee his son's security after he and his wife were dead.

"I wanted to get some equity, to leave something behind for Roger."

He became a workaholic, spending long nights at the office, and, usually, at least one weekend day, too. He made money and spent it; he got a title on his door, but had little feeling of inner peace. Because the future loomed as a threat, not as a promise, he took out enormous life-insurance policies. One year, their value totaled $400,000.

Nor was there much of the traditional family support systems for either of them. Our mother's family was three thousand miles away, separated not only by space but by my mother's continued practice of withholding information about Roger from them. In the traditional telephone conversations on Thanksgiving and New Year's Eve, when we would gather by the telephone to talk to Nanny and Grampa and Joey, our mother would say, "And Roger is just fine. He's doing wonderfully."

On our father's side, there was his mother, who came out to babysit with her grandchildren every Wednesday, giving our mother a day off so that she could go "into town" and have dinner with her husband. A short woman with powder-white skin, Grandmother Meyers died in 1952 when Roger was four and I was nine. We were told that she had died of "yellow jaundice." She had, in fact, died from the complications of cancer; but the word cancer in those days, like the phrase mental retardation now, carried a stigma and a curse with it. "Polite" people avoided saying it.

Our parental grandfather was a help, too. I remember him as a dapper old gentleman with matching pocket handkerchief and ties who liked to smoke Webster cigars and draw pictures of birds. He'd sit holding Roger on his lap at his window on West End Avenue and sing songs from Romberg's *The Student Prince* (a schmaltzy show that still chokes me up).

Today, the idea of respite care for parents of the retarded is an established principle, a part of the notion that it is better to keep kids at home, rather than warehouse them, but that the parents also need a break now and then. Trained babysitters for the retarded drop by, so that the folks can get a night on the town. Back then it was the grandparents, friends, or nothing.

From our father's sister, several years his senior, there was no such support, no such affection. Brother-sister arguments of long standing, which had erupted and subsided during their mature years, broke down for one final time during Roger's early life: My father asked his sister to babysit with Roger, and she refused. They have not spoken since.

My mother has always loved to entertain, and there were parties, sometimes as often as once a week. Usually they took place on Sundays, whipped together with a chafing dish, a beef Stroganov recipe, and wit. Some of the parties had themes: There was an Oriental party where everybody had to wear Chinese costumes and false mustaches. Our father wore an embroidered Chinese robe with a winged dragon on the back, which he'd bought in China in the 1920s. There was an "Everything You Are" party in which guests had to come as their spouses. The winner was the man who came wearing his wife's bathrobe with hair curlers on his head.

"When *Auntie Mame* was published, I figured we'd beaten them to the punch," my mother said. "I've always loved parties, always loved people." She also loved to decorate the apartment, changing the foyer and living room every so often to make the apartment look "French Provincial" one time, "Red Lacquered Chinese" the next. She refinished furniture and was the envy of her friends.

Roger was never hidden, as is often the case when parents are ashamed of their retarded child. He was always made a part of the family's life.

"Your parents were patient, decent, gentle, and civilized with that problem," Richard Wincor, a family friend and New York attorney, recalls. "There was never any closeting of the child."

"I took him to the circus and the rodeo, just like I did with you. On Saturdays, I would take him to my office with me, and at lunch I taught him to say, '*L'addition, s'il vous plaît*' ["Please bring the check"], just like I did with you," our father said.

"Whenever we could we took subway rides, because Roger loved those trains so much. I'd park the car down by Jamaica Avenue, and we'd take the El into Manhattan. We could ride for hours on it. We'd go to the tropical fish store, and he'd pick out fish for the aquarium."

Two decades before the concept of giving the retarded as many everyday experiences as possible was developed, my parents and others like them were following common sense and human instincts by trying to integrate—however stumbling the attempts—the retarded into the community.

My closest friend in those days of boyhood was Michael Baer, a kid with curly brown hair and a pug nose who lived directly above us in apartment 401 and with whom I frequently communicated by using a spoon to rap a code on the bathroom water pipe. He recalls:

"My earliest remembrances of Roger are visual images of a, maybe, two- or three-year-old, curly-haired blond, almost milk-complexioned boy, with little motor co-ordination and little movement. . . . From time to time he breaks into a smile or laughter where the expression changes completely. . . . An ongoing view or perception was that he did not respond to us. That he did not jump up, he did not join in, that, unlike other little brothers and sisters, we didn't have to chase him away. He didn't join. . . . I remember no grief in the house over Roger. I remember him being treated as Roger. To me, at our age, he was not like us. Yet I don't think I ever made the conscious distinction that he was in any way different . . . that Roger was less, that Roger was wrong. . . ."

His sister, Kathy Baer Porsella, has a somewhat different recollection of those days. "You guys could tease him. When you were playing, you didn't want him around. Roger had a runny nose a lot, and you called him 'candlestick.' You didn't want me around either, and the two of us would get left out."

The Baers had the first television set among the families in the building who had kids, and we would gather together each night sitting cross-legged in front of the screen, watching "The Howdy Doody Show" and, on Tuesday, the real treat: Milton Berle on the "Texaco Star Theater."

"Roger didn't have the patience to sit there with you kids," Harriet Baer, Mike and Kathy's mother, remembers. "He wouldn't come up very often."

It was not only that Roger didn't have the patience for TV, but something else as well—being around kids his own age who did not have his handicaps made him nervous, and conscious of not being able to compete as well. Even so, my mother tried to invite other children Roger's age over to the apartment as often as possible to relieve the loneliness that plagued him for many years, and which was not fully alleviated until he married Virginia.

His best friend in the early 1950s was Andrea Weissman Hart, then his age, five or six or so, and now a graduate student in clinical psychology at Clark University in Worcester, Massachusetts.

"I'd go over to the apartment very frequently after school. I had no idea Roger was retarded, none whatsoever. He was my friend and we played together, including sexual games—explorations. That was how we learned about our bodies.

"I remember once we were playing with toys, and I broke something. I think it was a rubber knife. Your parents, particularly your father, started yelling at me. They said things to me that I didn't understand, but it all came down to: How could I do this to Roger, didn't I know that he was different? But I *didn't* know he was different until they pointed it out to me. After that, because of the way they treated me, I didn't want to go back there."

Andrea has a very detailed and correct recollection of our apartment: the small back bedroom Roger and I shared, the location of the rooms, and the placement of the furniture. With her professional training in pscyhology, she is used to exploring her memories of the past. What she does not have, however, is a recollection of me.

"I don't think I knew you existed. You were never around,

and I don't recall anyone ever talking about you. Whenever Roger was there the conversation was always about him. I don't think I knew that Roger had a brother."

Perhaps that was because Roger didn't have an older brother so much as a miniature second father.

From the time that Roger began going to physicians and consultants, it seemed to me that I carried a five-hundred-pound lead weight around in the front of my brain. Never out of my mind was the idea that my brother was retarded, needed special attention, needed special care, and that I had to provide some of it. I could never escape the unspoken instructions: "Be kind, be courteous, be concerned, be careful." I never took much control of things and was never willing to challenge authority, because if I yelled at my parents for slights real or imagined or if I told them (or even felt) that they were crazy, wrong, mean, or whatever, they implied to me that such actions would really be a rejection of my brother. So I kept my mouth shut.

Such developments were not lost on them, however. "I worried about you, about the effect Roger was having, would have on you. You were a part of the family; we needed you to help with Roger, but even just worrying about what effect it was having on you tore me up," our mother said.

My role in those days was someone who was always around to help care for Roger. That was my mother's phrase. My father called me his "good right arm." Roger himself called me "Dad" before he corrected himself and called me "Bobby." Such concepts retarded my own development, since the center of my concern was my brother and not myself.

I was exceedingly mature and responsible. I would come home early after school just to be around in case my mother needed "help" with Roger. I do recall that the apartment had a fragile quality to it. We could not be too much of a roughhouse gang because of the implied delicacy of Roger, or quite possibly, because of the implied fragility of our parents' emotions.

I never felt I dressed like a kid, never felt comfortable with the clothes I wore, never felt I knew how to act as a boy or a teen-ager. I was a little man. I was five when Roger was born, seven when the fact of his retardation began to have an impact. I think that one reason I have been able to surmount that is that my own personality was formed by the time Roger was two, before the impact began, and so my personality was only covered up by my new role as his guide and aide, not destroyed or never allowed to develop at all.

Barbara de Pasquale, who was a mature high school student when I was still in grade school, thinks the necessity of entertaining myself led me to become a writer. "You always did a lot of reading, and then worked at short stories. You had to amuse yourself; that was the way you did it. I wasn't surprised to learn that you went into writing."

Reading was an activity that I could "do" by myself. It broadened my horizons and gave me a sense of participation in adventures I felt other boys were having but I wasn't. The transition to writing, creating something for others to read, was, perhaps, a logical consequence.

On Monday, October 23, 1953, at the age of five, Roger entered the kindergarten class at The Queens School, a private co-operative school located several blocks from our apartment in Kew Gardens. With our mother's tutoring, he had made great strides. He was walking and running, able to struggle into most of his clothes (though tying a shoelace was then an insurmountable task); listening better to people and making responses of his own, although he still had a short attention span and was still fascinated to the point of distraction by car wheels, tops, flushing toilets, and anything else that moved fast. At The Queens School's ungraded classes, he was integrated with children his own age, got teaching in reading and numbers, and that sense of socialization that is so important to a normal life.

"There were no classes for him then at public schools," Millie Racheny, for many years a teacher and administrator at the school, recalled. "Oh, there were classes for the retarded, but all they did was teach them to sit at attention for three hours a day, and then they sent them home."

On the first day of school, our mother walked Roger the two blocks to the yellow brick building (one of the last structures designed by architect Stanford White). At the steps of the school, Roger (like many other children on the first morning of school) burst out crying. But very quickly he came to see the school as a home away from home, a place where he could be himself and share his experiences in a wider world.

"He was fascinated by the weather," John Pelzer, who was for many years the school's maintenance man, remembers.

"He would come up to me in the morning and tell me what the weather was going to be. He listened to the radio or watched the television, and he'd give a full report."

Once Roger was settled in class, he might listen to the teachers, color, or gaze out the window. "Several years ago we got a letter from him—after a space of twenty years!—telling us all about himself," Racheny said. "What he was doing, and how he was bored in the sheltered workshop he was then in because all it involved was packing things in small plastic bags, and he wasn't paid very much for it. But what surprised us most of all was the fact that he'd written, because when he was here he couldn't even hold a pencil."

When the stress of class got too much for him, Roger would "go to the bathroom," not to relieve himself, as school officials found out when they became concerned about his frequent absences, but simply to get away from the pressure. This is a trait that has stayed with him to this day: He will, at times, leave the floor of his restaurant job and disappear into the men's room, until one of the waitresses knocks on the door and calls him out.

"Roger always knew what he wanted to say, but because of his speech impediment, he'd stutter and get frustrated. His face would turn all white and he'd shake his hands in sheer frustration," John Pelzer recalled. "But he didn't let it stop him. No sir, he'd go up to a new child here, and he'd say, 'What's your name?', just like that."

Roger stayed at The Queens School for five years: two years of kindergarten, two years of first grade, and a year of second grade. The costs then were about $625 each year, plus deficit assessments when expenses outran income from tuition.

"He tried so hard; he really did. If you gave him a note to

take home to his parents, he'd hold it in his hand all day long, until the note became soggy and crumpled," Racheny said.

"At Christmastime he brought me an envelope with a little gift in it, and handed it to me in the morning," Pelzer said, sitting back in the chair as the memories returned. "All day long, he'd come up to me and ask, 'Have you opened it, John? Well, open it!' He wouldn't leave me alone."

That was the good part of his school experience—the sympathetic teachers and staff. The difficult parts were brought on by his faulty motor co-ordination, speech impediments, and mental slowness.

"It was very hard for him socially, because of his difficulties, hard for him to make friends—and how he needed them!" said Hattie Charney, the director of the school for many years. "He was a thin, fragile little boy, very sweet but very lonely."

"When the other kids would tease him, he'd start to cry," Pelzer remembers.

"Your mother was here a lot, too, helping with the bazaars and cake sales and other fund-raising events. She'd be here whenever we needed the parents. Your father, too, on parent-teacher nights, I can remember it as clearly as if it was yesterday. He'd sit right there," Racheny said, pointing to the chair I sat in. "He'd say, 'He's not retarded. I know he's going to snap out of it someday.'"

There was the old theme again—seek help for the retarded son who you deny is retarded.

"Your parents really tried very hard not to face it," Charney said. "They'd attribute his problems to one thing or another: maybe the language difficulties would clear up, maybe a new drug would be found; maybe another doctor or procedure. I'm not trying to fault your mother. She was a wonderful mother. She loved Roger and she gave him his strong ego which is what saved him. But we know now that love is not enough. Frankly, I don't think The Queens School was the best solution for him, but I don't know what was; in those days, maybe there wasn't anything else."

While my father could relieve his anxiety about his son by a competitive business attitude, my mother had only her home to turn to. When the planning for the theme parties and wallpaper changes was over, she turned to something that relieved the symptoms, though not the root of her stress; she started, she says, to drink.

"I wouldn't drink heavily, but I always looked forward to it, and I wouldn't miss the chance at lunch or dinner. It was social, but also something I needed." "Cocktail hour" became almost a figure on the clock, with wine or sherry eventually being replaced by martinis and daiquiris.

"Whenever I'd go over to your mother's house, the first thing that happened was I got offered a drink," Millie Racheny recalled. "It was friendly. I didn't think too much of it at the time, though you could see the pressure she was under. Once Roger came to school late, with his hair uncombed and looking kind of scruffy, and I thought, *Hmmmm*, I wonder if Roz had a bit too much last night. But that's a normal reaction to problems, and she was always a wonderful mother."

I have no recollection of my mother's drinking excessively, but I have sharp and specific memories of a lot of pill-popping. Barbara de Pasquale described it as "popping Miltown like peanuts." There were jokes about it: "God, I need a Miltown," my mother said, with mock horror but also underlying fierceness, the way some people say, "God, I need a cigarette."

On my mother's night table was a bottle of Miltown, and on my father's a bottle of Maalox.

Like their concern for Roger, my mother's drinking was not something to share with anyone else. "When I heard about it years later, I said, 'Well, when did that happen?,'" said Margaret Woodman Husted, my mother's dearest friend at that time. "I just had no idea, and your mother and I talked every day of the week. Not a day goes by that I don't think about her, now, and I just don't recall that."

There are secrets and secrets, and it is difficult leading a normal life when so much is done in hiding.

4

POEMS FOR CHILDREN

BUBBLE GUM

One day I went to the store.
I bought bubble gum for 5 cents.
The bubble gum man says its yours.
It was two bubble gum sticks. In my mouth
I chew and chew and do tricks with my bubble gum.
I chew and blew a big bubble then POP!
It smeared all over my face.
It feels sticky.
I roll the sticky bubble gum with my tongue.
I put it in my mouth and I chew and chew,
    and do tricks with my bubble gum, it's fun!

CRACKER JACK

Cracker Jack came from my
Goodie pack. I eat it as a snack.
It went crack and smack.
I got a prize,
It was two peers of eyes.

THE PIZZA STAND

One day Liza ate her pizza
at the pizza stand.
She met a girl named Pam,
Who ate her pizza, at the pizza stand.
Liza and Pam were as big as a ham,
Eating their pizza at the pizza stand.

—ROGER MEYERS

Sometime in the 1790s in the woods of France, someone put a knife to the throat of a young boy and cut. The boy, who was probably about five years old at the time, was abandoned by his attacker, possibly a relative. The wound, however, was only superficial and the boy survived, living off nuts and climbing trees, his eyes darting around at the sound of a tree branch cracking.

In late September 1799, in the woods of Aveyron, three hunters seized the boy, believed then to be about ten or eleven years old, as he tried to climb a tree to escape them. He was taken to the home of a farmer named Bonaterre, washed and fed, but then he escaped again. After his second "capture" he was confined to local hospitals. A year later, in September 1800, he was sent to Paris.

This was the Paris that had idolized Jean-Jacques Rousseau, taking to its heart Rousseau's notion of the "noble savage," a primitive, uncivilized man. The sudden appearance of the wild boy from Aveyron confirmed the belief in masses of people who came to watch him cower in fear—here at last was the human beast!

In Paris, he was examined by Philippe Pinel, then head of a hospital for the insane. Pinel stated flatly that the boy was not a "noble savage" but a youth of profound mental deficiency—an idiot, in the phrase of the time.

One of Pinel's colleagues was a young physician named Jean-Marc-Gaspard Itard. Imbued with the spirit of youth and a belief in the equality of all men that had been such a rallying point in the French Revolution of only a decade earlier, Itard said that the boy was not mentally deficient at all, but only untaught. He asked for and received permission to work with him, which he did for five years.

The "wild boy" at the beginning of his schooling had no speech, but used only guttural sounds. He ignored gun shots fired at close range, but jumped when a walnut was cracked behind him. He could not understand the conceptual difference between an actual view of a mountain and a picture of it.

"He was destitute of memory, of judgment, of aptitude for

imitation, and was so limited in his ideas, even those relative to his immediate needs, that he had never yet succeeded in opening a door or climbing upon a chair to get the food that had been raised out of the reach of his hand," Itard wrote in 1801.

This great teacher then devised a series of exercises to "humanize" the *enfant sauvage* as much as he could. With Itard's infinite patience and the aid of a Madame Guerin, a nurse and housemother, the boy learned to use printed letters to make simple ideas clear, to differentiate among objects in a room, to express affection, and to use his mind.

The boy was named "Victor," because he most readily responded to the sound of the O vowel, although he never learned to speak.

"Unhappy creature," Itard cried one day, when his frustrations at Victor's deficiencies had gotten the better of him. "Since my labors are wasted and your efforts fruitless, take again the road to your forests and the taste for your primitive life. Or if your new needs make you dependent on a society in which you have no place, go, expiate your misfortune, die of misery and boredom!"

Hearing this, *and understanding it*, Victor's chest heaved and he sobbed and sobbed.

After several years with Itard, Victor ran away to the woods, was captured by gendarmes, and spent two weeks in jail. When it was recognized that he was the pupil of Itard, he was sent back to the doctor and his beloved governess, Madame Guerin. "Scarcely had Victor caught sight of [her] when he turned pale and lost consciousness for a moment, but, as he felt himself embraced and fondled by Madame Guerin, he suddenly revived and showed his delight by sharp cries, convulsive clenching of his hands and a radiant expression. . . . He appeared less like a fugitive obliged to return to the supervision of his keeper than like an affectionate son who, of his own free will, comes and throws himself in the arms of the one who has given him life," Itard wrote.

It is not clear from the great teacher's two reports on Victor whether the youth's mental deficiencies were caused at birth or were due to the prolonged time he spent wandering the woods of France, living off the land, plucking birds for dinner, and berries when he could find them.

Most professionals deduce from Itard's work that Victor was profoundly or moderately retarded at birth (and there is even one researcher who feels he was not retarded at all). Whatever the cause of his condition, the study of Victor, the Wild Boy of Aveyron, is the most famous of early attempts at helping retarded people to help themselves.

Carol Knieff, Roger and Virginia's counselor, and the thousands of other human-service workers like her, is in a direct line of spiritual descent from Jean-Marc-Gaspard Itard, the young physician who worked with Victor. Roger and Virginia Meyers and the other millions of retarded persons like them are in a direct line of spiritual descent from Victor, a boy who needed help to achieve his full humanity.

Between then and now, however, are decades and generations of social prejudice, ostracism, neglect, discrimination, and inhumanity, which have only recently started to be partially corrected. Although the patient teaching methods of behavior modification and ego construction which Itard used have been available at least since his time, their use stopped almost entirely in this country in the late nineteenth century.

In the 1850s, small fairly humane state schools for idiots and imbeciles (as the profoundly and severely retarded were called then) were set up in New York, Pennsylvania, Connecticut, Ohio, and Kentucky. The leaders in the field at that time were Edouard Seguin, a French physician who had been deeply influenced by the work of Itard, and Samuel Gridley Howe, a Boston physician who had worked with the deaf and blind. (Howe's wife, Julia Ward Howe, wrote "The Battle Hymn of the Republic" in 1862 on stationery from a mental-health commission.)

The concept of the schools was as temporary training centers for retarded persons, who would later be returned to their homes and communities. This was done with reasonable success. Gradually, however, the schools began receiving and accepting children whose families did not want them back, which increased their enrollments.

The physical size of the institutions began increasing, too—something that Howe first encouraged and then disavowed as "unnatural and very liable to abuse." At an 1866 dedication of an institution for the blind in Batavia, New York, Howe courageously questioned whether the place should have been built at all. "We should have as few [institutions] as possible, and those should be kept as small as possible. The human family is the unit of society," he said.

The belief apparently developed, however, that the schools could not help the retarded, who were, in truth, "hopeless." They might be victims of poverty or of "bad blood," and they might be deserving of charity and pity, but that was about all. The retarded became linked with crime, alcoholism, prostitution, and insanity. People began to think that the best place for them was away from other people. The schools, which originally had been built close to population centers, gave way to institutions which were constructed in rural areas.

In 1859, Charles Darwin published his *On the Origin of Species*, whose evolutionary concepts appealed to those in the field who thought they saw "feeble-mindedness" cropping up as a family trait. Eighteen years later, in 1877, R. L. Dugdale, a prison inspector, published a book called *The Jukes*, which tried to show the impact of environment on a poverty-stricken family. It was taken by some, however, to show the hereditary nature of antisocial tendencies, which were "always" found in the retarded.

At the same time, for unclear reasons, the notion also began growing that when the retarded were not busy planning the degeneration of society, they were busy fornicating. This ingrained even further the idea of strictly segregating by sex the inmates of the institutions.

An Austrian monk and botanist, Gregor Mendel, had quietly spent much of his life cataloging his breeding experiments with peas. The results produced what is now known as "Mendel's laws," which essentially hold that certain traits are genetic, inherited, and can be predicted once information about parent generations is known. Mendel's work was published in 1865 and ignored. In 1900, however, it was popularized by "modern" thinkers in this country, and picked up by educators and charity officers, who felt it gave them a scientific basis for what they had known all along: That mental retardation is not only a condition which breeds immoral conduct, but that the condition can be passed from one generation to the next.

Howe's concept of education on a temporary basis, which had been changed to long-term custodianship, was developing into complete warehousing of the retarded who, since they were "inherently immoral," did not need anything more than a bed and a bowl haircut.

In 1905, Alfred Binet, a French psychologist, developed a test for determining which French school children could handle a normal work load and which could not. The test was based on a selection of verbal and intellectual performance characteristics of children at various ages, and was used to determine an age-scale by which a person's ability could be measured against a norm. The Binet test, devised strictly as a measurement, was quickly misinterpreted in this country as a predictive yardstick by people who wanted to find out where feeble-mindedness was going to occur next. (The notion of an intelligence quotient or I.Q., using the Binet test, was shortly afterward developed by psychologists Louis W. Stern and Lewis M. Terman.)

In 1912, Henry H. Goddard, director of research at the Training School at Vineland, New Jersey, a private facility, published his study of the Kallikak family (the name is fictitious), showing alleged extraordinary feeble-mindedness, criminality, wantonness, and lewdness through several generations of the same family.

The eugenics movement, a terrible movement which believed that human traits could be controlled through selective breeding and that it was necessary and patriotic to do this unless society was to be destroyed by the retarded and feeble-minded, had started.

"Feeble-mindedness is . . . an uninterrupted transmission from our animal ancestry. It is not reversion; it is direct inheritance . . . society must end these animalistic blood-lines or they will end society," Dr. C. B. Davenport wrote in 1912.

Retardation was caused in 65 percent or 80 percent of the cases by heredity, Goddard wrote, and all you had to do to control it was lock up the hereditarily inferior.

However, feeble-mindedness was not something that was randomly distributed throughout society. Rather it was found almost exclusively in the lower classes, and quite often among foreigners.

Goddard addressed the National Education Association in July 1911 at a convention in San Francisco. He told the teachers of the nation's children that: "The method of preventing the 65 percent of hereditary cases is manifest without discussion. It is to prevent their being born. It is merely a question of time when the general public understands the tremendous hereditary force in this particular that we shall take the necessary steps to prevent this type of feeble-mindedness. . . . We must . . . either provide homes for such people where they can by no possibility procreate their own kind, or else we must by surgical interference make it impossible for them to perform that function."

By misusing the Binet test (and setting a pattern for continued misinterpretation that exists today), Goddard not only described the "idiots" and "imbeciles" he saw all around him, but a new class which he discovered: the "morons," or mildly retarded people, who might try to trick society and pass as nonretarded:

"He is a menace to society and civilization; he is responsible to a large degree for many, if not all, of our social problems."

The answer lay in segregation, sterilization, and prohibition against marriage. Laws mandatorily "asexualizing" the retarded were passed in many states; as of 1972, they were still on the books in twenty-four states. Until very recently, persons in institutions were strictly "quarantined" from contact with people of the opposite sex.

Such concepts were not seen as inhumane by the professionals at the time, because the retarded were also believed to be "moral imbeciles." Walter Fernald, superintendent of the Massachusetts School for the Feeble-Minded at Waverly, Massachusetts, once examined 1,463 persons at the Elmira, New York, reformatory and discovered that "73.9 percent conclusively had absolutely no moral sense, 15.7 percent had some moral sense," and the remainder were OK.

In 1912, Fernald recommended educating only half the population to the eugenic menace posed by the retarded, because, "We may deal with the other half of the community by our segregation and our sterilization propositions, or by other means," he said. Such was the degree of fright that had been stimulated by this "eugenics menace" that Fernald could actually say that half the American population was feeble-minded!

Although there was some belief at the time that sterilization would not work, it was not an idea that would die out. In the May 1929 issue of *Eugenics* Magazine, a man named E. Arthur Whitney wrote: "If we but apply the principles of heredity to human beings, then we may evolve a superior race and in so doing eliminate the social menace of those who are feeble-minded." He wrote that it was the "obligation" of the medical profession and social welfare organizations to promote "eugenic sterilization."

In 1931, a Dr. Butler, in a discussion with other eugenicists, said that, "If we could prevent the menstrual period, that alone would make the work with the low-grade girls in the institutions simpler and give better results."

Eugenics and social improvement were in the air. In 1933, in Germany, the Act for the Prevention of Hereditarily Diseased Offspring was passed, and 100,000 retarded persons and terminally ill persons were exterminated. It did not happen here, but that is just about the only thing that did not take place, as far as the debasement and dehumanization of the retarded are concerned.

History is not a dead letter; it is a living, organized set of beliefs passed from father to son, teacher to pupil, generation to generation. Those times are not that far away. My father was born two years before Goddard's book on the Kallikak family was published. My mother was born eight years after Goddard delivered his speech to the NEA meeting in San Francisco. The teachers who heard Goddard and Fernald and all the rest taught their pupils what they had heard; their students taught others. Some of these "taught" my brother or counseled our parents. Insult became injury. The medical profession whose members—Itard, Howe, Seguin, and others—had pioneered proven educational methods for the retarded, dropped to the sidelines in the first half of this century. Psychiatry and psychology came to the fore, deeming the retarded to be "sick" patients who could by definition never get well. Since mental retardation was an illness in medical terms, good health was the complete absence of mental retardation. Since intelligence could not be changed (it was falsely believed), since retardation was a fixed, static condition (it was falsely believed), there would always be illness. It was "helpless and hopeless."

The institutions became larger and larger, dinosaurs with few brains. From 1909 to 1949, the mean average amount of money spent on each person in U.S. institutions was $1.82 per day. The mildly retarded (the morons) were supposed to do work at the institutions to pay for the support of the others; the morons, in effect, were serfs.

If they were serfs and morons, then they probably would not care too much about comfort either. So they were hosed down all at one time in a tile-wall bathroom, the water draining into a hole in the center of the sloping floor. They were fed at the same hour, bedded down at seven at night, cared for by attendants who themselves were paid less than dog catchers and zoo keepers. Since they could not be cured of their retardation, they were given little help; the fact that they did not learn more was proof of their stupidity.

In the late 1960s, at the height of the institutionalization movement in this country, 190,000 persons were in state-run institutions. Millions more were subjected to society's abuses outside institutions.

The Layman's Guide to Psychiatry, a popular and inexpensive high school and college paperback textbook by James A. Brussell, M.D., was published in 1961 by Barnes and Noble. Brussell was then Assistant Commissioner of Mental Hygiene for the State of New York. He tells us that "morons can learn to perform simple, routine tasks, such as errands, distributing leaflets from house to house, washing cars, et cetera. Too often their suggestible and undeveloped minds are capitalized upon by criminals, who can easily train them to be killers. Morons are generally sullen and sulky, easily irritated but very responsive to flattery and gifts."

"We were taught in med school to recommend institutions. We all thought intelligence was an unchanging factor," said Dr. Richard Koch, a pediatrician who was one of the first in this country to publicly blast his colleagues for the horrible conditions that existed at the Willowbrook Developmental Center on Staten Island, New York, a facility built for two thousand persons in which six thousand were then "living."

In the 1950s, when physicians recommended putting Roger into a state facility, the one they recommended was the one that had recently opened on Staten Island, popularly known by the community it is in—Willowbrook. Our parents do not know why they didn't follow their doctors' advice, but they didn't.

Willowbrook was exposed to public view in 1972, when television reporter Geraldo Rivera and a camera crew documented scenes out of hell, scenes reminiscent of Buchenwald, scenes that once might have been found anywhere in the country—bent and broken bodies, urine and feces on the walls, moans and cries.

After a lengthy legal proceeding over Willowbrook, a consent decree filed in 1975 established the principle that retarded people had the right to protection from harm, to care, to the ability to walk around, to treatment, clean clothes, and curtains on the walls. Today, because of legal actions, the mildly retarded and the better-functioning people have been moved out, and the people who now remain (about two thousand in 1978) are primarily moderately and severely retarded. But what would have happened to Roger if he had been there? I put my question to Mrs. Rosa Brown, a therapy aide who has worked at Willowbrook since 1967.

"I saw lots of mildly retarded people come in here. They were able to walk, to talk, to eat on their own, and to go to the toilet by themselves," she said. "But they lost it. They stopped doing that, stopped eating by themselves, stopped walking, afraid to talk, going in their pants whenever they had to. There was no help for them then, nothing. I fed many of them myself," she said.

I called Niels Erik Bank-Mikkelsen, at his Copenhagen office. He is one of the great men in the field of retardation, the man who developed the normalization principle which led to so many changes. I put the same question to him. He answered, "It is hard to say; there are many factors, but there is a word for it. . . ." There was a pause, and then he said, "He would have been invalidated."

I don't know why my parents did not follow the best medical advice of the time, but I have never loved them more for it.

5

FOG

When fog is here I feel lonely
For you, dear.
The fog's watervaper is the tear of love.
Sometimes fog might cause harm,
But I will keep you safe in my arms.
When fog is here it hides me,
I can't see you.

But I know that you are there,
Cause God's love is everywhere.
Then all of a sudden, the sun peeks through,
The fog goes away. Everything looks new.
Now I can see you, on a bright clear day.

—ROGER MEYERS

Virginia Rae Hensler was born at full term on May 25, 1951, in Indianapolis, Indiana, the fourth of four children.

According to medical records, Virginia had gotten turned around and bent over during the birth process, and was lodged inside her mother in such a way as to prevent a smooth delivery.

"A Caesarean [section] should have been performed," said Virginia's father, Benton Hensler, M.D. "But the operating physician didn't want to do one—they weren't in fashion then—so forceps were used instead."

As he wrestled her from her mother's womb, the physician

injured her head with his forceps. "It was like a tug of war, my momma says," Virginia told me.

As a result, Virginia's left side is weaker than her right. She limps, has a speech impediment, scoliosis (curvature of the spine), and is partially blind in one eye.

"She didn't breathe for forty seconds after she was born," said her father. Although he says that Virginia's retardation "did not" have a significant impact on him, he has not seen his daughter since 1974. He did not attend her wedding or acknowledge the invitation.

The irony of the forceps accident was that the medical profession then believed that the use of forceps at birth could eliminate the traumas associated with Caesarean sections. Today that belief is no longer widely held. According to Warren Pearse, M.D., head of the American College of Obstetricians and Gynecologists, the use of Caesarean section began to replace forceps in problem deliveries about ten years ago.

Because of the traumatic nature of her birth, Virginia's condition was noted at once. She lived for the first few months in the hospital and then was sent home. She was a tiny child with a sweet disposition, and her mother doted on her.

"I wanted to find the best place for her, some place where she would get all the help she could use. I was afraid I couldn't give her everything she needed," her mother said.

This attitude was consistent with medical practice of the time, which held that specialized facilities were the best places for retarded children. If the child was kept at home, his or her condition might otherwise handicap nonretarded family members. For Virginia's mother, the decision to institutionalize Ginny Rae was a wrenching one, which kept her awake at night, and caused her much grief and sorrow in her own personal life.

"I wanted to do what was best for her. I really did. One of my best friends said what I was doing was selfish, but I really think what I did was best," said her mother, whose voice often catches as she talks about her daughter.

Because of her husband's successful medical practice, they

were able to consider expensive private residential care. Three years after Virginia was born, she was placed by her family in the Woods Schools, a well-known private facility founded at the turn of the century on four hundred acres of rolling countryside north of Philadelphia.

From 1954, at the age of three, until 1965 when she was fourteen, Ginny Rae lived at her "home-away-from-home." The buildings included a rambling Civil War era structure with white columns where Virginia lived for several years. It had a reputation among local historians as having been a waystation for the underground railroad, which helped runaway slaves escape from their owners.

"It's difficult having handicaps," Virginia told me, making sure that I understood that she was Virginia, now, her adult name, and not Ginny, the name she went by as a child. "I had to practice making myself understood. I had to practice the D, T, and L sounds, and learn how to swallow properly."

Her parents (eventually only her mother) would drive or fly the several hundred miles to the school to visit her, often having to rush to arrive before 7 P.M., when the children were put to bed. This early bedtime, a common practice in residential facilities for the retarded, was for the convenience of the staff. It is now frowned upon in some quarters because it denies the retarded their right to normal daytime hours.

As a child Virginia was a "little mother" to the other children. She helped them dress themselves; she took toys and schoolbooks out of the closets for them, and she tried to show others how to read and write. Even as an adult, living at a facility in California, she would let her own dinner get cold as she helped feed others. As a fiancée, she had to practice not being so motherly with Roger, who encouraged her to do things for him—such as his laundry—but then felt hemmed in when she did.

Virginia was a favorite of the housemother of that period, Grace Van Sant, a cherubic, white-haired woman who now lives in retirement near the school. "She called me 'Momma Grace,' and was the sweetest thing. She was a worker at anything, repeating words until she got them right, trying to make herself say it correctly. She would mediate problems between the other children, calm things down, and just by her example encourage them. Some of our children wouldn't eat because their food had lumps in it, or wouldn't wash their faces because they were afraid of getting soap in their eyes. But Ginny Rae would urge them to eat, or she'd wash her own face, and they'd see they could do it without hurting their eyes. I used to nip in the sleeves of her dresses, because one of her arms was so much thinner than the other. I used to feel guilty sometimes that I didn't spend more time with her, but she didn't have the problems the other children had, and she was so good," Mrs. Van Sant said. "I remember so well her brushing her own hair, then I'd braid it and tie the braids with ribbons, and when she'd run, her hair would go bobbing up and down."

As a wedding gift, Mrs. Van Sant sent Virginia a small red, blue, and black jug which the housemother had won at a fair when she was just six or seven years old. "I told her I was getting older, now, and didn't want to have these things around me anymore. So Ginny wrote back and said, 'Oh, Momma Grace, you're not getting older, you're getting better. Anything you send me I will treasure.'"

Holiday visits with her real family at their home were highlights of Virginia's life. "We baked pies in the summer, with fruit from the trees," Virginia said. "My brother would take me driving in his car, and I'd sit on his lap, holding the wheel. I didn't like to go mountain climbing because of my leg. I was a little lonely, but I don't want to talk about it."

Once when she arrived home for a visit, she went straight to her sister Carol's room. "She just stood there looking around, her hands on her hips, shaking her head," their mother remembers. " 'Well, it's about time I came home; this room is as dirty as it can be,' Ginny Rae said." Then Virginia cleaned it up.

"I really didn't know her then, really didn't know much about her," says Carol MacIntyre, her sister. "She would come home and be treated like a Kewpie doll; then she'd go back to the Woods Schools. She was supposed to be getting help, but at the age of six she couldn't eat a sandwich. I really didn't get to know her until we both lived in the same city. Virginia and Roger would come over to babysit with my first child, Scottie, who has cerebral palsy. Virginia was good with him, so good with him, and it was then that I got to know her, and see how much she understood. She told me, 'Don't worry, Scottie will learn things; it will just take him a bit longer, as it does with me.' Without her I would have had a much harder time accepting him."

Back at school, Virginia worked on her diction, on controlling her tongue movements, and on working within her abilities. If she was lonely, she kept it to herself. She talked about her family constantly. She was regarded by the staff as a happy and well-adjusted girl, who, nevertheless, became disturbed by changes in routine, and who cried whenever her teachers tried to discuss her handicap with her. One of her greatest frustrations in the third and fourth grades was trying to make her handwriting more legible. But she was not able to master the art.

When I told Virginia that I wanted to visit the Woods Schools in order to research this book, and that I would need her written permission before anyone there would speak with me, she got so excited at the idea of my going back to her home of eleven years that she squealed with delight. Then she took out a notebook and a pen, and made a point of telling me she would "write the note with my left hand, even though I'm right-handed, so everyone there will know how much my silly left hand has improved."

"*To the Woods Schools: I give my permission for anyone to talk to Bob Meyers about me. [signed] Ginny Meyers,*" she wrote with her left hand, a triumph if ever there was one, then ripped the page out of its spiral binding, and handed it to me.

During her stay at the Woods Schools, a consulting physician had her wear a leg brace on her left leg during the night in an attempt to straighten the leg muscles. Grace Van Sant remembers Virginia determinedly buckling on the brace and orthopedic shoe every night, stubbornly refusing offers of help. "She was going to do it herself," Mrs. Van Sant recalled.

But once Virginia's frustration overcame her sweetness and tolerance. "I threw the brace out the window. It didn't break anything because the window was open," she said.

When Virginia first arrived at the Woods Schools, the monthly tuition was $350. When she left eleven years later, the monthly tuition was $650. Over a period of eleven years, Virginia's family spent approximately $66,000. Those figures do not include the costs of visits or her travels back home.

Today, many of the special classes and training procedures which were used at the Woods Schools and other expensive private facilities are now available through public-school systems in this country. The Education for All Handicapped Children Act, passed in 1975, requires that "free, appropriate" education for children ages five to eighteen be in effect by 1978, and that it be available to children up to the age of twenty-one by 1980. The quality of programs which school systems receiving federal money must develop, and the impact of those programs on people needing them, remains to be seen. But the law, and the intent, did not exist before.

Virginia was taken out of the Woods Schools in 1965, and spent the next year or so in another private facility in the East. But her mother, who had moved to the West, wanted her daughter closer to her. By then, no longer married to Virginia's father, her mother researched all the private schools in the western United States. She chartered an airplane to fly to each one. The facility that was chosen had opened a year earlier. Virginia lived in Unit 1, the circular dormitory to which my brother moved on March 31, 1970, where they met.

Virginia is atypical of other retarded individuals in that she lived for so many years in private residential facilities. An estimated 10 percent of persons perceived to be retarded right now live away from home, in one of the 239 public residential facilities throughout this country, or in one of the more than 400 private residential facilities or group or community homes. The current philosophy in the field holds that living at home is best for most retarded people, because there they will be subject to a wide variety of "normalizing" experiences that they couldn't get anywhere else.

But twenty-five years ago, when Virginia's and Roger's parents were trying to find help for their children, and were trying to find a way to hold on to their own lives, which were buckling under this unexpected pressure, they didn't understand and had difficulty handling the advice that was offered time and time again by physicians in the field: "Institutionalize them!"

James Clements, M.D., head of the Georgia Retardation Center, is a pediatrician who shed this light on the attitudes of his medical colleagues who for years have held back on development in the field: "Physicians are trained to be administrators. They make a diagnosis and then they delegate the authority for carrying out the prescription. They like solutions. When the only solution was warehousing, that's what they recommended."

Frank J. Menolascino, M.D., former head of the National Association for Retarded Citizens, said, "Doctors are trained in acute medicine. You've got a broken leg? I'll fix it. Something's bothering you? Here's a pill. But it used to be if you told them your child was retarded, they'd shrug and say it was helpless and hopeless."

Menolascino and N. Karen Kelly published an article in the December 1975 *Nebraska Medical Journal* in which they surveyed attitudes of sixty physicians toward recommending services for the retarded in the Omaha, Nebraska, area.

The results showed that one out of two physicians was unfamiliar with the local parent organization for retarded persons, and one out of three was unfamiliar with the regional system of centers for retarded persons—the only two groups in that area that deal exclusively with the retarded.

Eighty-one percent of the physicians interviewed said they referred parents to the local Visiting Nurses Association; yet only three percent of the parents surveyed said they had ever received such a recommendation. Forty percent of the parents said they had been told by the doctor to institutionalize their retarded child, though none of them did that.

The attitude of physicians toward the retarded is crucial, since physicians are the traditional heads of the health-service systems in this country.

Yet, today, there is no mandatory teaching of information about mental retardation in U.S. medical schools, according to a spokesman for the American Medical Association. As the Omaha survey indicates, the fact that there are services available does not necessarily mean that physicians will know of them or recommend them, if they do. The AMA has an excellent handbook for physicians on the subject, but it wasn't published until 1965.

"Pediatrics did not begin to play a role in the field until the 1930s," said Robert E. Cooke, M.D., a member of the Joseph P. Kennedy, Jr., Foundation, an organization concerned with mental retardation. "Until then, psychiatry tended to get all the unexplainable problems. There was a preoccupation with diagnostic categories, as well as an inability to differentiate between mental retardation and mental illness; for example, schizophrenia. So everything got lumped together."

Cooke credited the interest of pediatrician Arnold Gesell in the development of normal children as one of the signs of positive medical interest. "Since, if you're interested in how normal kids develop, you're also going to learn a lot about why kids don't develop normally." He also credited Grover Powers, M.D., a world-respected physician and teacher at Yale, with fostering interest. "Years before any of this had ever been formalized in theory, Powers was encouraging his students to look more closely at mental retardation. He also thought the retarded ought to stay with their parents whenever possible." Cooke was one of Powers's students.

"Look, there's a message here," said Harold S. Barbour, Ed. D., who is currently head of the Woods Schools (he arrived there after Virginia had left). "Physicians don't like irreversibility. They want to see things change, heal, and become whole again. If they can't do that, they tend to wash their hands of the whole problem. We try to tell them that we work around the problem, that we try to compensate for it."

One person who agrees is Virginia Meyers.

"Being retarded means it's twice as hard showing people how we are, that we can live like normal people. We're not that dumb; we're slow-minded is all. You can see how far we've come."

 **6**

GOD'S IMAGE

You and I was inside the image of the
Sun's rays of light that shineth
Up to God so bright, opening the clouds, making
You and I warm, filled by his love.

God fights off the darkness that we were in
Before, after the closing of the clouds door.

We are in the image of God that's overflowing
love. It's the image of a dove, the symbol of
God's bird, his wings that flys like angels around.

We hear the sound of a bell ringing, people singing
of love and laughter.
There's no disaster in God's image, his power
Fights it off more than an hour.

Where is there love? Look into God's image
and you'll find it there, over the air and
over the rainbow and all around us.

—ROGER MEYERS

In the spring of 1956, our family moved from one section of Kew Gardens to another. We gained two more rooms and a patio, as well as access for me to Forest Hills High School, which was the better school in the area.

Roger was then eight; I was twelve. He was attending classes at The Queens School and I was a student at Russell Sage Junior High School. Our father was in the advertising business in Manhattan, and our mother was usually at home, alone with those fears she rarely expressed.

A grimness and intensity entered our lives then, as Roger's slow development became more and more obvious, especially as I began to accelerate in school and he did not. Gone were those nutty parties and the frequent changes of decor. The pressure of living with a son they loved and didn't know how to help was getting to my parents. There was a great deal of tension in the air. During meals at the dinner table, the only sounds were of forks scraping on plates, my father clearing his throat, my mother bent over looking at her food, her head down.

Once a friend of mine from school was over for a Saturday lunch, and he announced to my parents, with all the certainty of a teen-ager, that since there was no God, he was therefore an atheist. He was met with dead silence.

When he had left, my father erupted in rage against this stupid, ignorant, arrogant, impertinent little s.o.b—who did he think he was? My father was not a devoutly religious man, but the child was a convenient target for his pent-up anger. I remember wanting to smash the blue-patterned serving dishes with my fist. But I didn't, of course. I didn't do anything but keep quiet. I was a dutiful son, a "second father," and I wasn't allowed to disturb their already troubled world. Roger's retardation was a net that restrained and retarded us all.

My father was always on the lookout for a job that would "give him equity," so that he could put money aside for the future Roger would face when our father and mother were dead. In the 1950s, and for all the decades before, there were no state or federal funds for the retarded, except those spent to warehouse them.

In all of his searching for "equity," however, my father never took the one classic step that most middle-class people take to get themselves some "equity"—he never bought a house.

I strongly suspect that the reason my parents never bought a house is that a house represents responsibility and commitment, and in Roger they had all the responsibility and commitment they could handle. I suspect that the emotional pressure of wanting to help their son, and being afraid they wouldn't be able to, prevented them from thinking the logic of the financial situation through. So they took the short-run gain of paying rent in order to keep all their options open for Roger. The only equity they ever developed was their own resiliency.

On September 29, 1956, I celebrated my Bar Mitzvah, the Jewish coming-of-age ceremony. At the party in our apartment later that day, Roger asked the rabbi how you reached God. The rabbi said you prayed. Roger asked if that meant that prayer was like a rocketship, since God was in heaven and heaven was a long way away. The always-emotional rabbi, voice suddenly choked, agreed that prayer was indeed like a rocketship. Then he rushed from Roger's room in tears.

Roger shortly thereafter announced that he wanted to go to Sunday school, "just like Bobby did." There, the other children quickly proceeded to taunt and harass him, mocking his speech impediment and physical and emotional difficulties. When the religious-school principal and teachers said there was nothing they could do to control their students, my father angrily withdrew Roger from the class, and told me recently that "that was the end of my dealings with organized Judaism." Not until 1975 were classes started for retarded Jewish children in the New York area.

Not knowing what to do, my mother spoke with a relative who was active in the Christian Science Church, a religion whose theology of quiet acceptance of all people, based on the premise that each person, whatever his condition, must be perfect because he is formed in the image of God, held great appeal to her.

Roger began attending Christian Science Sunday school classes, encountered no difficulties from his classmates, and has been connected with Christian Science churches ever since. Roger and Virginia now attend Christian Science services each Sunday. They are picked up and delivered home by nearby congregants.

Soon after we moved, our parents were able to take Roger out of The Queens School, whose tuition they were having difficulty paying. They enrolled him in one of the earliest of the public-school classes for slow learners in New York City. In addition, they provided extra tutoring for him in reading.

"Your mother said it always made Roger feel extra special if he knew something the other kids didn't know," recalled Evelyn Springer Strauch, a down-the-hall neighbor who came in regularly between 1956 and 1958 to tutor Roger in reading for 50 cents an hour. "So I also tutored him in French."

One suspects it also made my parents feel extra special if their slowly developing son could speak French phrases, even if he was stumbling over English.

"Curiously, he never stuttered when we'd repeat the days of the week, the names of objects, and things like that in French. But he usually stuttered during his English lessons," she said, possibly because there was much greater pressure to correctly repeat words in the language he used every day. "Roger was a sweet, lovable little boy who liked to be hugged. Frankly, I didn't know that he was retarded until I read about it years later in your series. It was just that he wasn't coming along quickly, though the other son was."

Her brother, Gerald N. (Jerry) Springer, was a school buddy with whom I shot basketballs and shared secret thoughts about the mysterious and self-possessed girls on the school bus. I had not talked to Jerry in twenty years, and discovered that on November 8, 1977, he became mayor of Cincinnati.

"You always seemed a helluva lot more mature than the rest of us. At home I always heard, 'Why can't you be more like Bob? Why can't you be more like Bob?' At school you were active in theater, while I was out shooting basketball," His Honor said several weeks after his election.

I remember my father beginning to be overwhelmed by the doubts and fears that gnawed at his life. He began to slash out at the closest target; his humor turned to sarcasm. But Jerry Springer has a different recollection of him. "He was always so confident, so in control. Once at a party for my sister, the electricity failed in the building. Most of the people at the party were like my parents—immigrants, Europeans—and there was much confusion, running around, wondering what to do. But your father made everyone feel at ease; he took care of things."

My academic career has always been undistinguished, marked by a report-card phrase that has always haunted me:

"COULD DO BETTER." I believe I deliberately held myself back so that I would not too greatly outdistance my brother, who had trouble keeping up. Once that habit of self-restraint was learned at home, it was applied, as a matter of course, in other areas.

I held myself back socially in those days, too, not being as active with girls as other guys my age, not "dating" as much or bringing friends home from school. The memory of my father's reception of the teen-age atheist stayed in my mind.

In the ninth grade, the last year of junior high school, I decided to run for office. I wanted to be president of the class, but I calculated that to win at all I would have to run for an office no one else wanted. Therefore, I ran for class treasurer, something of a joke since math classes gave me fits. I later failed every science class I took in college, and was unable to balance my personal checkbook until the development of hand-held calculators in the 1970s. Taking the election as lightly as I did, my classmates elected me.

I was seeking recognition and I was seeking independence. Both were becoming increasingly difficult to find at home. There was love and pride and concern for me, but there was also a growing concern on my parents' part that as I became older I would leave behind my duties as my brother's "second father," my father's "good right arm."

I have the feeling my parents didn't want to see me grow up. My interest in writing was met with concern and disapproval. "We want you to do whatever you choose to do, *but* . . . Writers—especially novelists and playwrights—don't make any money. Most go years before being published. You'll starve. You'll never be happy!" (Most of all, though it was, of course, unstated and even unthought, yet powerful and persuasive to them—"You'll never be able to take care of Roger when we're gone.")

"Why don't you become a lawyer or a teacher? You can always teach, and write on the side." This traditional advice was always followed, two days later, by my father quoting George Bernard Shaw: "He who can, does. He who cannot, teaches."

In high school, I became active in the theater club, because it was an easy way to find recognition as well as read the dramatists—Shakespeare, Shaw, Ibsen—whom I loved. It was also a group in which misfits were tolerated, if not appreciated, and I was beginning a period of life when I felt I stuck out like a walking sore thumb.

In *Henry IV*, Part I, Prince Hal says:

> Yet herein will I imitate the sun,
> Who doth permit the base contagious clouds
> To smother up his beauty from the world,
> That when he please again to be himself,
> Being wanted, he may be more wonder'd at
> By breaking through the foul and ugly mists
> Of vapors that did seem to strangle him.

Those words for me were a shield, a motto, a statement. That was how I saw myself, for years afterward, covered over by clouds, waiting for the sun (or son) to break through, waiting for recognition. The works of Shakespeare helped me survive this period, when my brother's mental retardation was having as great an impact on us as on him.

In his pre-teen years, ages ten, eleven, and twelve, Roger expressed his developing (but frustrated) interest in girls by pinning their pictures up on his walls, writing poems about them, fantasizing about having girlfriends, talking about girls he'd known as a little boy, and by spending daytime hours at home involved with his "art work"—sketches of buildings and structures, many of them imitations of photographs, and on free-hand crayon drawings of dark-haired women, with elongated faces, eyes sunken, pinched mouths. Often these women had tear drops on their cheeks—our mother.

With enough intelligence to recognize his difficulties, Roger became hesitant about speaking out, fearful of failing. To protect their son, my parents worried about pushing him. Sometimes this closed off avenues of experience.

"Mr. and Mrs. Meyers are both concerned about Roger's future, his schooling, etc.," a report prepared for a physician stated in late 1958. "They both appear to be bright people who have gone through the gamut with this child and would, this examiner feels, make the best use of a 'straight-from-the-shoulder' opinion about their child. It has, it would seem, been long overdue. . . ."

The report evaluated Roger's I.Q. at 58, down considerably from the 75 he had received when he was two years old (and would again achieve when he was in his twenties).

The constant evaluation of him by physicians and others may have caused Roger pain and embarrassment (he shrugged noncommittally when I asked him if this was so), but it eventually produced in him a slick ability to slide off questions and an ability to manipulate the questioner in order to give the picture Roger wanted to give—a picture that put him in the best possible light. Virginia does this too, though less so than her husband.

Soon there was another residential move, this time in early 1960 to Manhattan, to a wonderful old high-ceilinged apartment on 76th Street and Riverside Drive (by coincidence, it was the same building my father had lived in as a child, nearly thirty-five years earlier).

The living room had a view of the Hudson River, and at night the George Washington Bridge seemed decked in a necklace of green lights. Roger and I shared a bedroom, but there was a maid's room, off the kitchen, and this is where I spent most of my time. These were fractured days. Our mother and father had accumulated a two-inch stack of medical reports and evaluations, a medicine chest full of tranquilizers, a liquor cabinet too quickly emptied, and not much else.

They were getting older, my father turning fifty in 1960 and my mother forty-one. The family fortune had not been made, their own personal expenses did not decrease, and good healthy chunks of money had been spent on Roger only to produce contradictory results, or predictions they couldn't bear. Their oldest son was getting ready for college (where would the money come from?), their youngest son talked over and over about people he'd met when he was three, four, and five years old, and listened incessantly to children's records.

Roger was attempting to make a life for himself. He was

attending special classes each day at William J. O'Shea public school in Manhattan, walking the half-dozen or so blocks from the apartment to the schoolyard, usually dressed a little too warmly (this was a burden our mother saddled us both with, preparing for arctic storms in April), carrying his lunch in a brown sack (he got ripped off for money and sandwiches by the school toughs, just like everyone else), and making friends with the burly Irish cop who acted as the street-crossing guard. Roger has always made some friends wherever he has gone.

Across from our building was Riverside Park, a strip of land sloping down to the banks of the Hudson. Sometimes Roger liked to go there after school to watch the boats sail down the Hudson, to watch the teen-agers playing ball and (in the summer) flying kites, to sit and bask in the sun.

It isn't clear exactly how it happened, but a man tried to sexually assault him one day. A stranger made an introduction, there was conversation, an uninvited groping, and Roger became frightened and ran away.

"When he came home and told me what had happened, I got hysterical," our mother said. "I collapsed screaming and crying. I didn't know what to do. I wanted to call the police, but I couldn't, I wasn't able to."

She paused a minute. "So Roger did. He dialed the police, gave them our name, address, and phone number. Up until then, I didn't even know he knew how to dial."

No arrest was ever made.

As they had always feared, his unsuspecting nature had put Roger at the mercy of others. But as they had also always suspected, he had more potential than he had ever shown. It took one to bring out the other.

Robert Perske, former director of the Greater Omaha Association for Retarded Citizens, calls this "the dignity of risk." Simply stated, it means that to overprotect a retarded person to such an extent that he is denied everyday experiences is to deny him a part of his humanity.

In one anecdote that Perske tells, the personnel at an institution were unable to find a severely retarded boy who had run away in subfreezing weather. The boy was eventually found—by his retarded colleagues, who had in desperation been asked to join the search.

Perske has movingly recounted the story of how some retarded adults in Germany outsmarted the Nazis who had come to cart them off to the gas chambers, and how others, crippled and unable to survive on their own, gave away their treasured possessions and prayed before the exterminators arrived.

"Recently I've realized that we have to add the idea of 'courage' to the idea of the 'dignity of risk,'" Perske said. "Just living a regular life is an act of courage for many handicapped people. How do you get upstairs? How do you dial the phone? If we overprotect them, we strip them of all chance for success. Handicapped people have really got to be seen as having a lot of guts."

Another area in which the retarded are continually underestimated is in their ability to conceptualize. One day, while shopping with our mother, Roger lingered by the candy counter, fascinated by the Jujy Fruits, the Hershey bars, the lemon drops, the Good and Plenty boxes. He took a box of candy, intending to go find his mother so she could pay for it.

"But the lady behind the counter thought I was stealing the candy. She yelled at me and made me give it back," Roger said. "I started to cry."

Fifteen years later, married, and a job-holder, Roger went to the movies with his wife to see *Forever Young, Forever Free,* the story of two African boys, one white and one black, who come to New York City seeking the medical treatment that one of them needs. Aliens in a foreign land, they stumble over customs familiar to everyone else. They can't understand the language that is spoken, they can't make themselves understood.

Roger Drake Meyers suddenly found himself crying. "I could identify with that," he said. "It made me think back to the candy counter." Unable to tell his wife directly why he was crying, he said only that he missed New York. Ever the faithful wife, Virginia Meyers also started crying, saying she missed her home, too.

As Roger told me this story, what struck me was the use of the word, "identify." That is a conceptual word; it implies an intellectual comparison between past and present. Such abstract reasoning is usually thought—by others!—to be beyond the reach of the retarded. Roger had identified with that scene because he remembered his past and could tell me about it in the present.

In the summer of 1960, Roger, growing tall, with fair hair and a ready smile, went off with a great hurrah to camp in New Hampshire. It was one of the great experiences of his life, one he still talks about. There, under sympathetic tutelage, he worked on his studies, practiced his diction and pronunciation, swam, and went horseback riding—an activity in which he surprised many of us by his excellence and sense of presence. In later years, it was with a touch of pride that I realized that he was a much better horseman than I, and that for once I was emulating him in my desire to excel.

He won ribbon after ribbon, competing against children his own age and of normal co-ordination.

A picture of him at that camp shows Roger determinedly trying to kick a soccer ball. He is somewhat unbalanced, his wrist slightly bent inward, dressed in oversized dungarees, with his tongue stuck in the left side of his mouth, and his eyes on the ball—he is *trying*.

Paul Stern, who vacationed at the camp, where his wife worked as a nurse and where his children were campers, recalled:

"Roger never dared to say NO when a kid abused his kind disposition. I found him on all fours with a boy riding on his back. Roger's knees were already chafed and bleeding from the exercise." The memory was clear to Stern after twenty years.

This has always been a problem for Roger. For the longest time, he had a hard time believing that anyone would want to take advantage of him, and the attention was worth more than the chafed knees.

"One day Roger confided to me that he was terrified, because one of the counselors had caught him as he tried to hide a dead rat in his cabin. He intended to bring the rat to the 'nature hut' as a specimen, because he wished to be 'first in nature,' but now he was sure he would be expelled from camp," Stern said.

Roger attended summer camps the following two years, each year improving his horsemanship. He made enormous progress in physical co-ordination, stamina, and in appreciation of how to control the enormous animal on which he sat. He could post, trot, canter, and jump low hurdles. He became proficient in grooming and saddling his own horses, and was a willing sweeper of stalls, though he complained, naturally enough, about the flies.

The question then and later arose: Could Roger live his life on a farm or a ranch?

"We thought about it a great deal," our mother recalled. "He was comfortable in those settings; he could handle the work if given supervision, and the people didn't torment him. We once talked with a woman who owned a camp, and asked if we might pay her for Roger to live there when he was older. She was interested at first, but, eventually, she decided she was getting too old, and she didn't know what would happen to the place after she was gone."

Our parents' idea of settling Roger on a farm was in the mainstream of much traditional thought about placement for the retarded. Early in this century, many state governments established their residential facilities for the retarded on large farms that were well removed from the general public. The notion that retarded people could perform complicated technical work was yet to come.

In 1960, my father lost his job, a victim of a rash of cutbacks in the advertising industry. With the shadow of my brother's condition becoming almost a specter and with Roger's future looming ever more bleak on the horizon, my father's frustrations, irascibility, and anger increased. He did business-consulting work, but our income level still wasn't back where it had been. Savings were broken into and expenses were cut back. A new phrase crept into the vocabulary: "for the sake of the family." Where once I had been a second father, and a good right arm, I now became a homogenized part of the larger unit, but during decision-making periods did not exist as an individual at all. The family was the viable unit, one that centered around the question of what would happen to Roger.

College began to loom as something that would break up "the family." My father, whose pride in me has always been boundless, began debunking it: Your college education is coming at exactly the wrong time. Ninety-five percent of all college teachers don't know a thing they're talking about. You can get a good education anywhere.

In my senior year in high school, I sat down with the New York *Times* Sunday theater section one day, made a list on lined yellow paper of which off-Broadway theaters had shows that were closing, took that list down to Greenwich Village, and began knocking on doors. My theory was that if a show was closing, another would soon be opening in its place, and maybe the new producers would like some free help. If I could get that, then I could later trade on it for a paying job during college. Much to my shock, I was taken on by the Provincetown Players, a semi-professional group performing Gilbert and Sullivan operettas, which worked out of the historic theater on MacDougal Street in which Eugene O'Neill's earliest plays had been performed.

My mother had not been employed since she did a World War II stint as a photographer's model. Then she'd donned Rosie the Riveter-type clothes for newspaper ads that encouraged the boys to get the job done over there so they could come on home. Now she decided to find a job to help financially support her family.

"We had a friend—a neighbor, really—and I asked him for any job I could get."

At the age of forty-one, Roslyn Willinger Meyers became a sales clerk, making two dollars an hour—the minimum wage. She went out every morning, with a smile and a shoeshine, to work at the posh New York specialty shop, Henri Bendel's, on West 57th Street—a store in which she could no longer afford to shop. She sold scarves and bracelets and impossibly pretty umbrellas to the "dear" and "darling" set, and at the end of the week paid for her family's groceries, putting the remainder aside for her younger son.

Our father was registered with an employment agency, and found the job he was looking for: a top management post with a firm in Miami. The salary was good and the potential was better.

"I wanted this to be my last job, the one in which I could find equity, so Rogie would always be taken care of," he said.

Even the move from Manhattan would suit the native New Yorker, because the pressure of New York was clearly having a negative impact on his retarded son, who seemed to prosper best under less stressful surroundings. They could start living like normal people again.

There was only one hitch: I would have to go to the University of Miami.

I refused. At my high school, Miami was known as "Suntan U.," the place blockheads went when no other school would accept them. I had actually joked with friends, long before my father's job offer had been made, that if I couldn't get in anywhere else, I could "always" go to "Suntan U." Miami at the time wasn't even recognized by Phi Beta Kappa, the scholastic honorary society. Miami was an expensive private school, whose tuition I knew the family couldn't afford.

But one horrible night, my father told me in the strongest possible terms that I *had* to go to Miami, for "the sake of the family."

So I went, for the sake of whatever was left of the family at that point, for the worst three years in my life. If I had been more independent, I would have done something to preserve my own identity—stayed in New York, joined the Army, something. But that was not the way I was.

7

A GIRL'S BEAUTY

(THE BEAUTY OF A GIRL)

A girl's beauty means a "very beautiful"
girl has all the lovely beautiful thoughts
within her. And that's what makes a
beautiful girl so "very beautiful!"

A girl's beauty means, "love," a "lovely girl"
has all the "beautiful" loving kindness within her!

A girl's beauty means, a sparkling girl has
all the best beautiful love within her—
A girl's beautiful face, hair, and eyes, are so
beautiful that they shine out her beautiful love
to you.

The beauty of a girl means, a girl's
friendship is too beautiful, that a girl is shining
her beautiful friendship love to you.

The beauty of a girl means, when a girl puts her
arm around her best friend, this means that she
is showing her beautiful charming warm hearted
love to you.

—ROGER MEYERS

On September 13, 1919, a daughter was born to a
couple in Brookline, Massachusetts. The girl, quiet and pretty,
was the third of nine children; none of the other children was
retarded. Her parents, who had become wealthy during their
lifetimes, were able to provide full-time care for their daughter,

who currently lives in the Midwest. The girl was Rosemary Kennedy.

To honor their oldest son, Joseph P. Kennedy, Jr., who had been killed in World War II, the Kennedy family established, in 1946, a foundation in his name. "We wanted to help children; that's always been a great interest of ours," Eunice Kennedy Shriver said. To avoid duplicating the interests of larger foundations, Mrs. Shriver and her husband, Sargent, traveled around the country seeking advice. Their conclusion was that "there was a terrific lack of work going on in the field of mental retardation. It was almost nonexistent."

Initially, the foundation established schools for the retarded in Los Angeles, New York, Chicago, and in Massachusetts. By the mid-1950s, however, Mrs. Shriver said that her father, former Ambassador Joseph P. Kennedy, "suggested we needed to refocus things." The foundation decided to emphasize service to the retarded, rather than simple care of them.

Interviews were then held with leading figures around the country: Richard Masland, M.D.; Joshua Lederberg of Stanford (a geneticist who shared in the 1958 Nobel Prize); Robert E. Cooke, M.D., of John Hopkins (who today is scientific advisor to the Kennedy Foundation); George Tarjan, M.D. (now at UCLA); and others. "We wanted to divert the interest of the leading scientists into mental retardation," Mrs. Shriver said. The Kennedy Foundation set up money for early research centers, the first scholarships in mental retardation for selected medical students, and clinical facilities for treatment and observation. The Foundation's influence was overwhelming in the early years, and it continues to be important. "Basic research is never enough. We need to get retarded people out in the public eye, so people will say that they're worth treating," Mrs. Shriver said.

When Roger Meyers was born in 1948, there was no national group organized on behalf of retarded people or their parents and friends. There were several local parents' groups, although none of them apparently knew about each other.

In 1933, the Council for the Retarded Child in Cuyahoga County (Cleveland), Ohio, was formed; in 1936 the Children's

Benevolent League was founded in Washington state; and in 1939 the Welfare League for Retarded Children was set up in New York state by parents whose offspring lived in the state-run Letchworth Village facility.

On October 12, 1946, Laura Sparks Blossfeld wrote a "Voice of the People" column for the Bergen (New Jersey) *Evening Record*, identifying herself as the parent of a retarded child, and suggesting that any other parents interested in forming a parents' group write to her, in care of the paper.

"I got three letters initially, then two more. At a meeting in Paterson, New Jersey, in June 1947, we had forty people show up. That was the start of our state's parent group," she said.

Her motivation was simple. "Whenever I went to the store or walked in the city, I saw children who were retarded. Yet the school system and the government said there weren't enough retarded children around to make it worthwhile to start programs. So I thought, if we could get together we could change their minds."

A nationwide survey showed that there were eighty-eight local groups of parents of retarded children in nineteen states with 19,300 members, in 1950, when my brother celebrated his second birthday, and his retardation and its impact were becoming painfully clear to our parents. Yet they had little or no impact on local, state, or federal governments and there was little communication between the separate groups. More important, people such as my parents did not know about the groups' existence.

At the end of September 1950, however, ninety persons met in the Radisson Hotel in Minneapolis, Minnesota, to form the first national group devoted to the aid of the retarded. The group's original name was the National Association of Parents and Friends of Mentally Retarded Children, which was soon shortened to the National Association for Retarded Children (NARC).

It is a mark of the newness of services for the retarded that the emphasis of the group, and its title, was on children. Not until 1973, as the children of the original founding members had grown up into adults, was the name of the organization changed to the National Association for Retarded Citizens.

During the 1950s NARC joined with several government groups in producing the first comprehensive work in the field: *Mental Subnormality* was published in 1958. NARC contributed to the research effort by raising $78,000 in a "Pennies for Research" campaign during a three-year effort; at the same time the much better known March of Dimes was raising millions.

During this time, the new national parents' group found a strong ally on Capitol Hill: Representative John E. Fogarty, a Democrat from Rhode Island who chaired the House Appropriations Subcommittee on Labor and on Health, Education and Welfare.

As recounted by Gunnar Dybwad, who was executive director of NARC from 1957 to 1963, and who is Professor Emeritus of Human Development at Brandeis University, the first not-so-gentle push for Congressional action in the field of retardation came on Tuesday, February 8, 1955, in Room F of the House of Representatives, in the hearing room of Fogarty's subcommittee.

HEW Secretary Oveta Culp Hobby was seated in front of Fogarty, answering questions on the subject of the aged. Suddenly Fogarty switched direction and asked the first of what have become known as "Fogarty Questions":

"What are we doing on behalf of these millions of [mentally retarded] children in this country?"

For the next ten days Fogarty grilled every top-ranking official of every bureaucracy whose agencies had anything at all to do with mental retardation. He learned that one "psychiatrist" was working at the National Mental Health Institute, and that the government was spending not more than $155,000 on the entire subject.

"The federal government is doing practically nothing in the field of mentally-retarded children," Fogarty concluded.

In January 1956, the NARC leadership presented a ten-point program to Fogarty. It emphasized community counseling and training with parent involvement, special school classes, as well as classes with nonretarded children, sheltered workshops, vocational training, day-care centers, and vocational rehabilitation, among other things.

With the aid of his colleague on the other side of the Hill, Senator Lister Hill (D-Ala.), Fogarty was able to authorize $750,000 for research and training programs. Until 1963, Fogarty's was the only piece of federal legislation in the field.

In 1958, the President of NARC, Elizabeth M. Boggs, Ph.D., was appointed by President Dwight D. Eisenhower to a panel developing issues for the upcoming White House Conference on Youth and Children to be held in 1960. One of the outcomes of that work was the NARC document, *Decade of Decision*, which contained many of the programs later backed by the Kennedy administration.

On October 17,1961, President John F. Kennedy established the first President's Panel on Mental Retardation. Mrs. Shriver was named a consultant, and is largely credited by people in the field as being responsible for its efficiency and eventual success.

Her husband, Sargent Shriver, who is also very active in the Kennedy Foundation, said that with the panel's existence Mrs. Shriver was able to do within the government much of the work she had been doing outside of it.

To prepare its reports, panel members fanned out across the globe, researching work that was being done elsewhere. In Denmark, they found what they thought of as a remarkable approach to dealing with the institutionalized retarded person. Instead of large, barn-like institutions, with their rows and rows of hundreds of beds, feeding schedules, and hosing-down periods, they found a series of small homes in which rarely more than three dozen retarded residents lived, usually in their own rooms, or in a room with one other person. The rooms themselves were attractively furnished, often decorated with personal possessions, which their families were encouraged to bring. Some of the retarded adults were married and lived with their spouses; others were single and had a social life with friends of the opposite sex. Some of the retarded adults worked and took public transportation to their jobs; retarded juveniles were in special classes designed to help them develop work skills that could be used in working situations.

"We didn't have a name for what we were doing," said Niels Erik Bank-Mikkelsen, who was then director of the Danish

National Service for the Mentally Retarded. "We were just following the law."

That law had been passed in 1959, in response to criticism from the National Association of Parents, formed only a few years earlier in 1951 to 1952. The parents' group (set up at almost the same time as its American counterpart, the NARC) had protested against large facilities, a "protectionist" attitude on the part of the medically-oriented administrators, and lack of education and job training.

"The heart of our Act was this expression: 'to create an existence for the mentally retarded as close to normal living conditions as possible,' " Bank-Mikkelsen said. "That is what we set out to do. Maybe it was easier here than in America. We are a small country; we have no slums such as you have; we have a homogeneous population, and a tradition of pride in our social services. Not everyone approved of what we were doing, you know. Parents liked the idea of their children being 'cozy' all the time; administrators thought we were taking authority from them. But we were able to do what we did."

In 1961, Bank-Mikkelsen, who had gone into the Danish Resistance Movement in 1944 as soon as he'd received a law degree from the University of Copenhagen, traveled to London, where he met Bengt Nirje, then the Ombudsman (or head) of the Swedish Parents Association. The two men exchanged ideas, and Nirje began implementing Bank-Mikkelsen's ideas in his own country. "We challenged each other," Nirje said.

"It is normal to be retarded, though we don't try to make the retarded into normal people," says Bank-Mikkelsen. "What is normal? Who can say? Any society that did not have retarded people would not be normal. All we try to do is help the retarded people live as normal a life as possible. "

Almost exactly one year later, on October 16, 1962, the panel presented its 201-page *Proposed Program for National Action to Combat Mental Retardation* to President Kennedy. The report stated that mental retardation "afflicts twice as many individuals as blindness, polio, cerebral palsy, and rheumatic heart disease combined. Only four significant disabling conditions—mental illness, cardiac disease, arthritis, and cancer—have a higher prevalence, but they tend to come late in life while mental retardation comes early."

On the day the panel presented its report, news bulletins related that the President had "a cold." Mrs. Shriver said she called Evelyn Lincoln, President Kennedy's secretary, to ask if the meeting should be canceled. "He said to come on over. Something was in the air, but we didn't know what it was. He gave us his full attention at the meeting." Later, Mrs. Shriver and everyone else found out what was "in the air"—war-game planning for the then-unannounced Cuban Missile Crisis was taking place elsewhere in the White House. "God, he was cool!" she said.

Drawing on what the panel had observed in Scandinavia and elsewhere, the report made recommendations in the field of law, medicine, residential facilities, federal expenditures, and government co-ordination. Many of its recommendations, following outlines from the NARC, the Kennedy Foundation, and other organizations, form the basis for agency and governmental departments' policies and procedures that are in effect today.

Shortly before the panel made its report, Mrs. Shriver wrote an article, which appeared in the September 1962 issue of the *Saturday Evening Post*, about their retarded sister, Rosemary. Mrs. Shriver also told the story of new developments in the field of mental retardation.

"Rosemary was a part of our family," Mrs. Shriver said recently. "We played tennis together; she took dancing lessons; one time Jack invited her to a dance at Choate. She was never hidden, but treated in a normal way."

In the article she told of how one mother's persistence in the face of rejection from the medical community had helped lead physicians to an understanding—and later, control—of phenylketonuria (PKU), which will almost always cause severe or moderate retardation if incurred, but which can now be diagnosed at birth and successfully treated with a simple diet.

She told of how a Pennsylvania engineer had developed a tiny valve for the treatment of hydrocephalus, or excess water on the brain, which causes retardation. The man had developed the valve because doctors told him one did not exist.

She told a story of hope, in simple, unsentimental terms. The article had an enormous impact.

My mother said, "It was the first time I remembered anyone in the public eye having written something like that. I thought it was wonderful."

On February 5, 1963, President John F. Kennedy sent the first (and only) message to the Congress that concerned itself, specifically, with the subject of mental retardation and mental illness.

In his message, Kennedy recommended two proposed Acts, which were passed by the Congress and signed by the President on October 24, 1963. The first, which became officially designated as Public Law 88-156, amended the Social Security Act to more greatly benefit the retarded and authorized funds for the individual states to begin planning their responses to mental retardation.

The second Act, which became designated as Public Law 88-164, provided construction funds for university-affiliated research centers and funds for the training of personnel in the field of special education.

Millions of dollars were soon appropriated on the federal level to implement these landmark pieces of legislation.

8

TEARS

Every tear drop has to fall
of someone's crying call
Lots of tear drops fall.

Every tear drop is rolling down
Someone's cheeks, full of lovely wet tears.
Tears are like the falling rain, coming
From the crying pain, from a broken heart
That never will be apart.

Look at someone's crying face, and you can tell
Tears are beautiful, lovely, sweet, and wet, like
Morning dew, and yet tears mean something. It's
Crying for me
I love you, I miss you, I want your help, more
My darling dear, through all these years.
When tears fall down on the ground, or whatever
They make no sound. They make it wet, wet, wet.

—ROGER MEYERS
(written for and about his mother)

Our family arrived in Florida in separate stages
during 1961. Our father had gone down in the spring to begin
his new job. Roger and our mother went down in June. I spent
the summer in the Catskill Mountains, my father having paid
three hundred dollars so that I could be an apprentice at a
summer theater. On September 3, my eighteenth birthday, I
joined my family in Florida.

The next day, in the swimming pool of the apartment

building in which we were living, my father gave me the news: The job was not working out. The man had a perfect Dun & Bradstreet rating, but there were legal problems with the firm which he did not like. He had decided to return to New York—did I want to come along?

I remember letting myself sink to the bottom of the pool. Roger and my mother were sitting in chairs by the poolside. He was looking very healthy and seemed more relaxed. My mother was wearing dark glasses and a straw hat on her head, the lower part of her face motionless.

I said I didn't know, that was something I would have to think about.

My father, who could not bring himself then to say how sorry he was for the way things had turned out, said he understood.

I did not return to New York. In fact I didn't go near the place for another ten years. A few days after the swimming-pool meeting, I lied and said that I had to stay at Miami because if I transferred back to a New York school in the interim, I would surely be drafted (which in retrospect would have been a good development). My father, fifty years old and beaten down by his attempts at managing situations which sometimes slipped away from him, sighed and accepted my decision.

What I was really thinking was that my parents were not in control of themselves, that they were making bad decisions based on hopes and fears rather than on facts and common sense. They were floundering, a common human plight, but if I stayed with them they would pull me down with them.

Curiously, Roger and I both worked out the same method of coping with our parents—we withdrew. I lied and said I had to stay in Miami. He increased his tendencies to tell himself stories, to re-enacting events he had experienced. He then played out all the parts and commented on them. He did this in his room, in front of others, or on the street. When I did the same thing later in life and put those stories on paper, I called it "writing fiction"; when he did it, it was taken as a sign of unusual social behavior, and added a layer onto the stigma he already carried.

Our mother decided that she would have to leave the traditional wife's role and enter fully into the business world. She went back to Henri Bendel's, working as a sales clerk, but now she did it with widening horizons. The firm had a business connection to the I. Magnin chain of specialty stores in California, with a major branch in San Francisco, near her hometown of Oakland. For my mother, who had lived in New York ever since her marriage in 1940, it was time to go home.

"There was nothing left for us in New York. It was expensive and unpleasant. Roger had prospered so much in Florida, I wanted to see him keep on living in a better atmosphere."

I was in school in Miami, miserable but enrolled in classes, holding down the usual variety of college jobs (library clerk, laboratory assistant, theater group technician), and not involved (therefore not a factor) in my parents' decision-making.

"I heard about an opening at the San Francisco I. Magnin branch and applied for the job long-distance. They could have hired anybody, but since I'd worked in New York, they said I could have the job if I went out there," my mother said.

She flew to San Francisco. Dad got a job as a draw-against-commission salesman of lingerie for a schlock East Coast firm, which agreed to pay his car expenses for the drive out. Sitting next to him on the front seat of the yellow 1960 Studebaker Lark was his youngest son.

"Moving to California wasn't easy for me to do, let me tell you. I was fifty, not exactly a young man, and here I was, about to go on the road again, calling on clients."

It took them about ten days to get from east to west. They left in a blizzard, then had smooth driving for much of the trip. "We'd sing songs, or Rogie would be the navigator, keeping an eye on the maps." Roger would sit upright in his seat, watching the telephone poles fly by the window, sometimes talking to himself, or when he got excited, shaking his hands between his knees until his father gently put a hand on his son's wrists as a signal to stop.

The furniture stayed in storage in the East, and the family

moved into a furnished apartment. Soon Roger began attending special classes at Marina Junior High School.

Our father quit the lingerie job almost as soon as they arrived. Then, unable to find a job he wanted in San Francisco, he sent out several letters to firms based in Los Angeles, four hundred miles to the south. One of them responded immediately, and he was hired to work with the advertising agency for a major retail drugstore chain. Mother left I. Magnin's to go with him.

In Los Angeles, they tried another furnished apartment. "It was really a tacky place with some hippies playing rock music all night long. Roger was not in school, but would sit on the front steps of the building all day, shaking his hands and talking to himself. In an atmosphere such as that, the manager told me Roger was a problem! He said we would have to leave because he was 'creating a disturbance' when he sat there. I told him to stuff it, that a lot of my friends talked to themselves. We left."

Our mother again decided to get herself a job, to begin putting money aside specifically for Roger's future. She heard from a neighbor of a secretary's job opening up at a local government agency. She applied for it, quite nervous, wearing sedate clothes, and leaving at home all her clanking jewelry. She was on her best job-applicant's behavior, and was delighted when she got the job. There was one problem: She couldn't type.

Her solution was typical for a woman who had never finished high school, who had learned how to think on her feet all her life, who had learned how to get things done: She hired a typist of her own.

"I brought home work from the office at night, and she would type it up for me. I was earning the minimum wage, two dollars an hour, and sometimes after I got through paying the secretary there wouldn't be much left for me. But I knew the job had potential. I knew I could move up, and so the expense was worth it."

Naturally, the picture of the housewife/secretary who was so devoted to her minimum-wage job that she took her work home pleased her bosses, although they could never figure out why this "secretary" only took dictation in longhand ("I couldn't take shorthand either"), and never produced finished copies of their letters until the next morning.

Then a combination of circumstances developed for which my mother *swears* she was not responsible: in the best tradition of 1940s college musicals, strange things began happening to all the people who were directly superior to my mother.

"One of the women broke a leg, I think it was on a skiing trip. Another got a divorce and decided to leave town. Somebody else just quit. Pretty soon I was the only one left, and I was only a secretary."

Naturally, with such a heavy burden upon her shoulders, and wanting only to do the best job she could, she proposed to her boss that another secretary be hired.

Only this time the secretary would be *her* secretary, and she herself would no longer have to "tie herself down" with standard secretarial chores such as typing and shorthand. She could, instead, concentrate on expanding the office and bringing in more business.

The ploy worked. My mother became manager of her division, earned a salary of $18,000 annually, and supervised a budget of more than $95,000.

At the bank down the street from her office, she walked in with one of her first salary checks and opened up an account. Printed on the bank book was the legend:

Roslyn W. Meyers
The Roger Account

In 1963, Roger began taking classes at Emerson Junior High School in the west side of Los Angeles, tucking his study books under his arm each morning and walking the half-dozen blocks to the school. He was prospering from the change in environment, becoming more calm and sure of himself as, in his teens, he could haunt the record shops in Westwood Village, pay two dollars for a Saturday afternoon movie, and walk home licking an ice cream cone without a fear of getting mugged.

Now that they were settled in Los Angeles, my parents asked me to rejoin them. Having nothing to keep me in Miami, and feeling that family life had stabilized somewhat, I agreed. In January 1964, I enrolled at the University of California at Los Angeles to continue my studies.

It had been more than three years since we'd all lived under the same roof together. We had all changed, in ways that made my parents' cherished notion of a permanently united family— three adults supporting the fourth—impossible to realize.

Each of our parents was now working full time, which meant that each of them came home from the office dead tired. Roger at sixteen was terribly, terribly lonely. When he was not in school he would watch endless hours of television, read his children's books, and rely on his phenomenal memory to make conversation—which became confusing and disheartening for our parents, since Roger was committed to recalling his past, and they were troubled by his constant dwelling on events that were at least a decade old.

I was twenty-one, a college junior, sexually experienced (something my parents had difficulty handling), trying to play catch-up as a transfer student while I plotted what I would do after college.

We got on each others' nerves. We were in each others' way. The television was too loud; money was short; my textbooks were too expensive. Roger was always in his room playing records.

A solution was found: In March 1964, Roger moved to a residential facility for the retarded south of Los Angeles, for which my parents paid $250 a month. State funds for such fees were available for the first time under legislation signed by President Kennedy—a sign of the changing times. But it is an imperfect world, and red tape prevented my parents from gaining access to them.

"I didn't want to go at first. I was afraid the kids would be rough and the teachers strict," Roger said.

But his parents persuaded him that "it would be best for

him" (our mother's phrase, unknowingly echoing the words used by Virginia's mother in describing why her daughter was placed in the Woods Schools shortly after birth).

"We hoped he would find friends there, and that he could start a life of his own. We had to admit that what we had to offer him, even as his parents trying to do the best we could, wasn't enough," our mother said.

It was the first time Roger had ever lived away from home (with the exception of three summers in camp), and it was not a good experience.

The facility, like so many others for the retarded, was located near the outskirts of a very small town, which offered very little in the way of real-life experiences. The managers originally promised that they would be setting up riding stables, and that the residents would be in charge of caring for the horses, saddling and grooming them, and that the fees for such services would help support the facility.

Such a concept fit in with the traditional notion (which is not widely held now) that all the retarded can do is care for nonhuman creatures. This concept, however, was all that my parents had besides hope, and it fit in with their traditional view of the possibilities.

But it didn't work out that way.

"There were stables all right, but all Roger did was clean them out," our mother said. The promised riding academy never materialized; nor did the fees for boarding horses. By locating the facility as far from society as possible, and by implicitly saying that all the retarded could do was take care of subhuman creatures, the facility was basically saying, "These people are different." The implication was that the difference was a negative value judgment against them.

The stables that did exist, however, were poorly ventilated. So hordes of flies regularly swooped from the stable area into the residents' living quarters. In the summer time, when the residents were "fed" outside, they were "fed" in an area that attracted flies in droves. I remember visiting Roger one day and being unable to finish my lunch because of the swarming insects.

To make financial ends meet, the facility secretly took in temporary wards of the county's juvenile-court system. But kids who've had to learn their smarts on the streets, who measure prowess in stolen hubcaps, or who are used to getting attention in troubled homes by slamming doors and breaking dishes are not the kind of people who are going to fit in smoothly with retarded people who are not, necessarily, emotionally disturbed.

The lumping of mentally ill people with the mentally retarded is a backward remnant of the days when medical and social knowledge was unable to distinguish between the two. People in the mental retardation field now fight vigorously whenever the two concepts are linked, precisely because of past experiences.

But at that facility, which had all the proper licensing from the federal and state governments, this outmoded and inhumane concept was being applied, primarily because the managers needed the money the court system would pay them to temporarily house these delinquent youngsters.

The resulting mixture of juvenile-court kids with the retarded was predictably volatile: There were fights, rip-offs, harassment, and torment. One night, Roger packed a few articles of clothing into a small suitcase, opened the window to his room, and ran away. With him, ironically enough, was one of the kids sent over from juvenile hall, who hated the place (for different reasons) as much as Roger did. The two of them headed toward town, the classic runaway story, sleeping by the side of the road, with their possessions in their hands.

"The housemother called us that night, to tell us that Roger had run away. We stayed up all night, worrying, until the police found them the next day," our father said. Roger and the other boy were found unharmed, and Roger was fairly buoyed up by the experience. He was beginning to know how much he could do on his own.

Although Roger was out of sight, he was not out of our parents' minds. On the contrary, their active concern about him dominated their lives, placing them on the edge of tension that made laughter difficult and relaxation impossible. There would be periodic collect telephone calls from Roger. There would be requests for school books and reading materials which would be dutifully sent down, but always with the unspoken question: Why isn't he getting this kind of help from the facility? and, Will it do any good?

There was their own continued preoccupation with money, trying to stay even, paying off the debts accumulated from the difficult days in New York and the subsequent cross-country move, and the expenses of driving on weekends to see Roger, staying overnight, and buying him clothes when needed. Little expenses, niggling items, but all expenses add up.

There was their college-age son, a UCLA senior, who never should have returned to live with them. Having encouraged me to come to L.A. "for the sake of the family," it was now almost impossible for my parents to recall that since last seeing me, I had been living by myself in my own apartment, earning most of my own money, and conducting my own social life. Although I was promised my freedom of movement if I rejoined them, I believe that what they were expecting was an older version of a high school student, whose presence would restore their lives to what it had been.

My behavior toward them was at times hostile. I tried to have as little to do with them as possible. Often we didn't speak. I didn't hang around bars, but I didn't hang around the living room either. I kept to myself in my room, studying. Once, during one of those torrid love affairs that seem like a good idea at the time, I came home around seven in the morning, and didn't have to worry about talking to them because they didn't talk to me for days.

Graduation day on June 10, 1965, was none too soon for me. Three months later I had a fifty-five-dollar-a-week-job as a book clerk and a small apartment of my own. In July of the next year, the inescapable fact that Roger's residential facility was woefully inadequate could no longer be buffered by hope for change. The houseparents, drawn from the local community, given no training whatsoever, and steeped in prejudice, were as stifling to Roger's development as the punks who also lived there. "I called one housemother the Warden. She could have come straight from a Cagney movie," our father said.

Roger returned home to live with his parents, although they had no more information about how they would help him then they had had before.

The massive changes in the law and the infusions of money on the federal and state levels was beginning to reap some concrete benefits. Groups of parents, like my parents, veterans of the wars of frustration, were banding together in attempts to use some of that federal money for the construction of facilities for the retarded in their own areas. One such group was drawing up plans for such a facility to be located in California. Within the next few years these plans would lead to the construction of the residential facility where Roger and Virginia would eventually meet.

"Virginia was shy and withdrawn, but she began to open up quickly," recalled William T. Gray, the former director of that facility. Gray had met Virginia and her family in Arizona, where he was then working as a state officer in the field of mental retardation.

After her parents separated, the custody of Virginia, then a minor, remained with her mother. The enormous expense of the Woods Schools in Pennsylvania where she had lived for most of her life could no longer be handled by either of her parents. Virginia's mother contacted Gray, seeking advice, and he suggested the then-developing California facility as a possibility.

"I rented a plane and flew all around the West, checking out each of the different places," Virginia's mother said. "I thought this one had the most potential."

Because of the Aid to the Permanently and Totally Disabled (APTD) Act, added in 1967 to the grabbag of federal monies sent to the states, Virginia was able to qualify for a full cash grant, which covered all her expenses at the facility. She arrived in 1967, shortly after the facility opened. She was a slim girl who loved to help children and whose own self-image improved as she saw how much she could contribute to others.

"She would feed the profoundly and severely retarded at

meal time, putting the food on the spoon and helping them taste it. She did this while her own food was getting cold," her mother said.

Despite its good intention, the facility had little of the aggressive and success-oriented projects then that it later developed. Virginia could participate in arts and crafts, watch television, or, because of her comparatively high intelligence, act as an aid to those with more profound handicaps. But there were initially few or no community visits, recreational outings, and the like.

Virginia was also lonely, precisely because she was not as handicapped as many of the others around her and had few people with whom to share her life.

She continued to work on her diction, continued to talk constantly about her family, continued to delight in the few visits to their homes which she made on holidays, and continued to mother the little children who looked up at her with their bright eyes.

Virginia and her mother both thought she would live in such an environment for years, if not for the rest of her life. Although the attitude of some of the adults around Virginia was a babying one, at least, Virginia's mother thought, she's safe, the people there are sympathetic, and she's going to be happy.

Our parents were not yet able to be so hopeful.

9

A VALENTINE

1. A "Valentine" is a whole lot of fun! When you run after a
"Valentine."
    Kids make Valentines and "Valentine cards" Friendship love
to you, from their "lovely," "warm hearts"!

3. A "Valentine" is "sweet" because it's sharing "warm" "affectionate" "love," "loving friendship," and "kindness ways"!

4. A Valentine means "love," For it is the shape of a heart
That's overflowing very warm affectionate "love."

5. A Valentine is beautiful, a beautiful valentine has hearts,
that's sharing the parts of love.

6. A Valentine heart is overflowing joy and happiness for every
valentine's toy in boys and girls.

7. A Valentine says, "happy Valentine's day for loving kind
people "LIKE YOU!" Happy Valentine's day!

    Will you be my Valentine? Happy Valentine's Day LOVE,
Roger (Feb. 14)

—ROGER MEYERS

In the spring of 1968, the laboratory division of the
Federal Bureau of Investigation in Washington analyzed the
original copy of this poem to determine if Roger Drake Meyers
had also written an obscene letter to the eleven-year-old girl to
whom he had sent this poem. He had not.

In 1968, Roger was twenty years old, a handsome young

man with light brown hair whose parents knew that his need to be able to support himself, at least partially, was becoming stronger and stronger.

As Roger lived with his parents, there was very little employment training available for him. There were (and are) sheltered workshops in which retarded citizens do subcontracting work under supervision for government agencies and private companies, but they were quite far away, and lack of adequate public transportation made it difficult for Roger to get to them. The training received in such situations is often untranslatable to the general society, because those jobs don't exist anywhere else outside the sheltered workshop environment. Even when they do, the age-old discrimination against the retarded often keeps them from being hired.

Nevertheless, one sheltered workshop for cerebral palsy victims was located nearby, and my mother got them to accept Roger.

He began doing piecemeal work, stuffing parts into plastic bags, and earning fifty cents an hour. It was during this period he wrote to Millie Racheny and his other former teachers at The Queens School, complaining of the boring work he was doing, hunched over a bench all day, stuffing little things into little bags. No wonder he dreamed of being a rock star or a poet—anything to relieve the boredom!

On Saturdays, when his workshop was closed, Roger often walked a few blocks to the local YMCA. He sometimes went swimming there (in one of his summer camps he had successfully completed a Red Cross Life Saving course), though his concern about competing with nonretarded kids his own age or younger more often than not kept him out of the water.

The Y's maintenance man, with whom Roger would walk around, while checking on the men's locker room, the basketball courts, and the pool, let Roger help him make change for the Saturday afternoon swimmers who wanted to buy Cokes. The soft drink cost fifteen cents, so when someone handed him a quarter, Roger had to hand back either two nickels or one dime.

It is remarkable how little attention is devoted to the subject of the loneliness of the retarded. There is information on management of the retarded, residential care, vocational training, learning disabilities, significance of testing scores and educational modalities, the need for parental respite care, preschool counseling, and the like, but very little on the loneliness endured by people smart enough to know, like my brother and sister-in-law, that they are "a little handicapped" (Roger's phrase). Working at the Y gave Roger a chance to talk to people about the Beatles or Beach Boys, a chance to be with normal people his own age—not those so severely retarded that they could barely feed or toilet themselves, not those with periodic epileptic fits, not those who are emotionally disturbed, but young men and women, teen-agers, boys and girls, who lived in the community and liked to swim on Saturdays.

Although Roger liked being in the community, at least some members of the community didn't like him. "It wasn't her fault," he says of the girl involved in this episode. "It was her father's and mother's."

One of the teen-agers to whom he sold Coca-Colas at the Y was a pretty eleven-year-old girl with long blond hair, and a willingness to talk to the shy young man on the other side of the cardtable. Which she did in brief chips of conversation concerning music or Roger's "interest" in poetry or movies they had seen. Later, in her parents' comfortable home, she told them about the day's events, including her talks with "the retarded boy."

On January 24, 1968, Roger, always thinking ahead, wrote the Valentine's Day poem printed at the head of this chapter and gave it to the girl who always talked with him.

Several days later, someone else wrote something to the same girl—a vile, obscene letter replete with four-letter words, sexual suggestions, and threats. The girl's parents, rightly concerned about their daughter's safety, immediately notified the local police. Because the obscene letter had been mailed to the girl, the local police notified the FBI, which by law can participate in matters involving the use of the federal postal system for the mailing of obscene material or threatening letters.

Following the lines of standard police procedure, the local policeman obtained from the girl the names of her male classmates and (apparently from school officials) samples of the handwriting of those students. The local cop was also given Roger's poem, with some kind of an explanation from the girl about "the guy" who had given it to her. The samples were sent to the FBI labs.

It is here that the truly invidious nature of the "eugenics alarm" movement comes in, half a century after Henry H. Goddard proposed his pseudoscientific claptrap claiming to link mental retardation and "inherited" criminal tendencies.

The agent at the FBI, putting the obscene letter together with the fact that a retarded person had written the girl a Valentine's Day poem, went to our mother, in her office, and showed her the obscene letter, though politely covering up the four-letter words. "He asked me if I thought Roger could have written the letter. I showed him the obvious, that the obscene letter had been written in script, and Roger's poem had been printed, because he didn't know how to write script then," she said.

Not letting those facts stand in his way, the local cop then drove out along Santa Monica Boulevard to the sheltered workshop where Roger was employed. He flashed a badge on the head of the workshop, and said he needed to see Roger Meyers on "a police matter."

Roger was called away from his workbench, and, in a back room of the facility, interrogated by the armed policeman who was wearing plainclothes. "He asked me if I had written that letter, and I said no. He showed me words I didn't understand, and I said I didn't write them. Then he went away," Roger said.

When he got home, he was shaking. "He was afraid he was going to lose his job. He started to cry. He didn't know what was going on," our mother said.

As soon as she learned what had happened, our mother raced to police headquarters to protest, in person, to the chief of police about the conduct of one of his officers. "All I remember is going into that office and screaming my head off. I told him there was no need for that, that Roger had never shown any tendency toward things like that, that he couldn't even *write* script. I don't remember anything else about that meeting, because I must have blanked it all out while it was happening," she recalled.

The handwriting samples, which had been sent to the FBI's graphology section in Washington, D.C., were returned to FBI Special Agent John F. Morrison in Los Angeles. The results conclusively showed that the obscene letter had been written by the eleven-year-old boy who sat next to the eleven-year-old girl in their junior high school home-room class. The boy who wrote the letter was not retarded; he was "normal."

"It was my fault; it was all my fault, I should have controlled that cop better," Special Agent Morrison apologized to our mother later. "I knew he was going off on his own. He thought Roger must have done it because he's retarded, and the retarded are supposed to be 'different.' "

Roslyn Meyers did not tell her husband until years later of any of the events that had transpired. "I felt Roger was my responsibility, my burden. I didn't want to trouble your father with it. It was a weight on me, a terrible weight, but I felt I had to bear it."

To help her along, she turned often to her solaces: alcohol and medication. She was never a heavy drinker, but a constant one. The drugs were another way out, a way she calmed herself to whatever sleep she could get each night. Once, she received a call at her office from a neighbor who, by coincidence, was at home that day. "Roger was standing on the shoulders of high school students, using a stick to knock out street lights," the woman said. When our mother raced home, she found Roger, in his room, shaking with fear. "The students forced me into doing that," he said. "They tried to blame me, but it wasn't my fault. It was *theirs!*"

It was beginning to be obvious that if Roger was led into trouble, his sweetness and charm would not get him out of it. At the age of twenty, had any serious legal matter arisen (the street-light incident would have qualified as malicious mischief or disturbing the peace), he could have been treated by the courts as a minor, or as an adult, or—what would have been far worse—as a mentally retarded person.

As a first-time nonretarded offender on such a charge, he probably would have gotten a fine or a suspended sentence. As a retarded person, he might have been ordered "hospitalized" for "evaluation and treatment," the seemingly humane treatment that, in effect, would have been a sentence of indeterminate length in a "mental institution," a treatment (assuming he ever got out or got out in one piece) that would have been a punishment far worse than the crime.

Although there are retarded people who commit crimes (as there are nonretarded people such as lawyers, doctors, presidential aides, and at least one United States Attorney General), it is of interest that a recent study by Miles Santamour, a researcher with the Department of Health, Education and Welfare, shows that retarded persons, who represent at most 3 percent of American society, represent 10 percent of the total prison population in this country—a representation at least more than three times greater than their number in the general population. Santamour believes that this is caused, in part, by the difficulty that persons of limited intelligence have in assisting in their own defense, and the short shrift they are given by their own attorneys and the court system in general.

As dramatic proof of what happens when a retarded adult gets involved in an explosive situation, a young paralegal aide in a Washington area jurisdiction told me about a twenty-two-year-old retarded man who had just pleaded guilty to an assault charge.

The trial stemmed from the fact that a police officer, responding to a neighbor's complaint, had found the young man, whose I.Q. is 48, standing with a knife in his hand, while his mother and the mother's boyfriend backed away from him.

It turned out, however, that the boyfriend had on a previous occasion *fired a gun* at the retarded man, trying to keep him out of his own house. When violence started this time, the twenty-two-year-old had picked up the knife in *self-defense.*

Although he never did anything with the knife except hold

it, the judge in the case chose to exercise a new option available in Maryland designed to give a fairer shake to the retarded. He called in the paralegal assistant and gave her five days to find alternative residence for the young man, who otherwise would go to jail.

After getting rebuffed by the state's own agencies designed to deal with the retarded, the paralegal aide came to the realization that there were no state-supported *residential* facilities for retarded *adults* in the state, although there were indeed several large and overcrowded *institutions* for them. An elderly couple in the neighborhood eventually took the young man in on a temporary basis, and later a foster home placement was found.

One day during this period in the early 1960s, Roger was at the school playground, apparently singing to himself, when a group of boys surrounded him and told him to sing for them. They told him to dance for them at the same time, and formed a circle around him to make sure. He sang and danced in a jerky, off-key style. When he told our mother about this later in the day, her face drained of color. "They liked my singing," Roger said.

Our parents and Roger were then living in a wealthy, middle-class neighborhood, whose elected representatives were "liberals," the first to embrace environmental protection, opposition to the war in Vietnam, and other "progressive" issues. It cannot be said, then, that Roger was suffering because he lived in a neighborhood whose residents were socially backward. Exactly the opposite was true. If enlightened social attitudes were going to be found anywhere, in theory, they would be found around the corner and up the block from where my family lived.

But this obviously was not the case: Goddard, Fernald, and the other indicators had done their job well.

Roger handled these scratches at his personality by absorbing them within the overall context of his life: He shrugs now when asked about them. If he was troubled by encounters with "rough kids" at the schoolyard, he avoided schoolyards. If older boys liked to tease him, he focused his attention on the younger children of his parents' friends, to whom Roger was a kind, shy, nonjudgmental adult, and one whom they could manipulate for the use of his toys. They did not threaten him physically, an immeasurable relief.

One of the standard recommendations to our parents was to have Roger declared incompetent in a court, a fairly standard act which would have made the State of California his legal guardian. They seriously considered this only when they feared they were running out of time, energy, and options. They never did it.

Instead, more sheltered workshops in the Los Angeles area were discovered by our parents. Roger went to several, traveling by bus, doing piecemeal work at one for $1.05 an hour, at another for slightly more. He stayed as long as the contract continued, and then was let go when it ran out. Once he was traveling home by bus in the late afternoon and sat in the back, in the only available seat, next to a man with stubble on his face and rundown shoes on his feet. "The guy had a bottle in a brown bag," Roger said, and in the spirit of men in the working place, offered a swig to his new friend. Roger took it, and passed the bottle back. "We drank it all up. I think it was beer or something." Roger got off at his stop, went home, and fell sound asleep at six in the evening.

Roger had become a past master of Hoola-hoops, able to twirl them around his arms, legs, neck, waist, thighs, ankles, calves, and forehead. He could handle one, he could handle more; at this time twirling Hoola-hoops was his greatest accomplishment, and my parents acknowledged it. No sooner would someone come in the house than their twenty-year-old son would start showing off with his Hoola-hoops. They took painful if ambivalent pride in his ability.

Poetry was his safety valve, for his frustrations at not having a normal life, not having a girlfriend, and not having any friends. His poems at this stage do not have the quality and intensity that some of the later ones do; rather, they were an outpouring of his growing unhappiness and sense of uselessness and his desire, he says, to make people happy.

There was something else: Roger says it was at this time, in 1969, that "Dr. [Richard] Koch said I was retarded. I thought classes for exceptional children were what everybody went to. I didn't know there was anything different about me or the other kids at school."

We were sitting in the living room of his apartment, the one he would soon share with his wife, and my brother was telling me how he first learned of the central definition of his life.

"Our dad took me there [to Children's Hospital] for an examination. Dr. Koch said it; before that, I never knew about it. At the YMCA someone had said it to me and I said, 'No! No!' It made me mad. But that's why I work so hard to learn the things I don't know, and so become not retarded. Ten or twenty years ago I couldn't do some of these things, like long division. But I can now. As a matter of fact, I can make change."

Our father says that he had told Roger on several previous occasions that he was retarded. Our mother said the same thing (none of the specific occasions is remembered). But for some reason Roger remembers only the meeting with Dr. Koch, perhaps because by this time, a "developmentally disabled slow learner," he was able, at the age of twenty-one, to *understand* what was being said.

For Virginia, the traumatic realization that she was retarded came in a courtroom when she was a teen-ager, as a judge heard arguments involving her parents' divorce and subsequent support payments for her. "It was shocking. All that time I thought I was normal. I was shaking. I asked my momma if it was true, and she said yes, and then I knew. But I don't like to talk about it because it makes me cry," she said.

Roger and I were jagged images of each other. Though I had not yet started to earn my living as a writer, writing was a constant avocation done while working in bookstores, in motion pictures as a go-fer, and collecting unemployment. The more I wrote, the more he wrote; precisely because I was a writer, "I wanted to be a writer, too," he said. Things became particularly troubling for him in June 1968, when one of my short stories was accepted for publication, and Roger had nothing to match that.

Our parents, responding to his desires and seeing the commercial success of people like Rod McKuen who wrote sweet cloying lyrics that they felt were similar to Roger's, began asking me to help Roger get published. When I responded that I could barely get my own work published, they decided that the one thing Roger lacked was an agent.

By coincidence I was soon afterward accepted for representation by a literary agent in New York. Within days my parents began hounding me to get the woman to represent Roger as well.

I will never forget the night this happened, at a Thanksgiving dinner in a business club. I began to think I was going crazy. I was struggling to start my own career against a stream of rejection slips from agents and publishers whose kindest words were "good luck" and whose unkindest were that I should try another line of work, and my parents could talk only of Roger's need for an agent, so that his poems could be published in book form. When I joined some friends later that night for a drink, they said I looked ghostly white and stunned.

It was shortly after this that I told my parents I would no longer speak with them. I did not know what else to do, since I feared becoming trapped in their emotional whirlpool, and they were clearly not looking at me as the person I was. That period of silence lasted slightly less than a year. Eventually, I decided that my own mental health would be better served by my having parents I had trouble dealing with than by, in effect, having no parents at all.

"That was a horrible period in our lives, wasn't it!" my mother said, later. My father nodded in agreement.

 **10**

THERE'S NO NEED TO CRY

You've been doing so good in many things,
don't give up, don't listen to the bad and then
be sad. The love of your image will never ever last.
For it will keep going. Forget about the past
that your loved one has left you, cause you have to
know he's all right with God. Don't be shy.

There's no need to cry. For God will weep away
Your tears. God hast wept tears for many years.
For in His kingdom there's no crying tears, only
happy tears. God loves you, for your love has
Come back to you. What great joy.

—ROGER MEYERS

After Kennedy panel members discovered the work of the Scandinavians in the 1960s, Bengt Nirje, then head of the Swedish Parents Association for Retarded Children, was invited on a speaking and lecture tour of the United States.

A former literature student who had volunteered out of humanitarian reasons for service in the 1956 Hungarian uprising, and influenced by the anthropological studies of Ruth Benedict and Margaret Mead, Nirje had the belief that the retarded should no more be deprived of a chance for the normal ebb and flow of life and of the normal rhythm of daily existence than should anyone else.

In this country during 1967 and 1968, Nirje lectured at

universities, in Minnesota, Wisconsin, Nebraska, and at Harvard. He talked about the small homes (not large facilities) for the retarded in Sweden and Denmark in which citizens (not children) lived in their own rooms (not in beds in gymnasium-size halls) with their own furniture, personal possessions, pets, and, sometimes, their own spouses.

For recreation they went into the community in small groups, not in large hordes, so that their personal and physical handicaps would be noticed and stigmatized.

Nirje talked about plans for the then-upcoming conference *of* retarded citizens—not a conference *about* them—in which fifty retarded adults, ages eighteen to thirty, with I.Q.'s ranging from 35 to 70, *discuss* their own needs and desires. (This conference, held at Malmö, Sweden, in May 1968, is believed to have been the first conference in the world in which retarded people actively participated.)

In early June 1968, Nirje arrived in Washington, D.C., to write up his remarks for *Changing Patterns in Residential Services for the Mentally Retarded,* a publication prepared by the President's Committee on Mental Retardation. Nirje had only three days to write the article.

Working day and night in a fifth-floor office in the HEW-South Building with a view of the Capitol dome, Nirje put down in writing the results of the Scandinavian approach. When he wasn't satisfied with a draft of the article, he ripped it up and started again. A rotating staff of three secretaries was kept busy typing the material. Once he was interrupted with word that U.S. Senator Robert F. Kennedy had been shot in a Los Angeles hotel.

Even today, exactly a decade after its publication, it is impossible to read that landmark work—no more than ten thousand words long and taking up no more than fifteen pages—and not breathe a sigh of relief. The concept is so natural, so simple, the approach so decent and humane.

". . . Normalization means a normal rhythm of the day for the retarded. It means getting out of bed and getting dressed even when you are profoundly retarded and physically disabled.

It means eating under normal circumstances: Sometimes [in institutions] during the day, you may eat in large groups, but mostly eating is a family situation which implies rest, harmony, and satisfaction. A normal daily rhythm also means not having to go to bed earlier than your peers because you are mentally retarded, not earlier than your younger brothers and sisters, or not too early because of lack of personnel.

". . . Normalization means to experience the normal year with holidays, and family days of personal significance. Most people change their life situations and refresh their bodies and minds at least once a year by going on vacation. In Scandinavia, travel, including travel abroad, has proved meaningful and valuable even for the severely and profoundly retarded.

". . . Children should have available warmth of atmosphere, rich sensory accumulation and surroundings, and settings of proper proportions. . . . In child-care homes, turnover of personnel should be minimal, thus offering the children basic security and opportunities for identification of the stand-in parents. . . . It is, therefore, completely wrong to let mentally-retarded children live in the same institutions as retarded adults.

"The normalization principle also means that the choices, wishes, and desires of the mentally retarded themselves have to be taken into consideration as nearly as possible, and respected. . . . Normalization also means living in a bisexual world. . . . Mixing of the sexes according to the normal patterns of everyday society results in better behavior and atmosphere, as more motivations are added. And the mildly retarded sometimes suffer in a loneliness that has no sense, and, as others, they may be better off married.

"A prerequisite to letting the retarded obtain an existence as close to normal as possible is to apply normal economic standards: child allowances, personal pensions, old-age allowances, or minimum wages. . . . Work that is done in competitive employment, in sheltered workshops, or within institutions should be paid [for] according to its relative worth.

". . . It is important for the mentally retarded to have a right to equal opportunities for education, training, and development. . . . The self-image of the retarded must be built on letting him experience his personal abilities; thus experience of rejection and disregard creates confusion, stress, and unhappiness. . . .

". . . Application of the normalization principles has profound implications not only to the retarded but also to the public, to those who work with the retarded, and to the parents of the retarded. . . .

"Isolation and segregation foster ignorance and prejudice, whereas integration and normalization of smaller groups of mentally retarded improve human relations and understanding, and generally are a prerequisite for the social integration of the individual.

"Normalizing a mental retardation setting also normalizes the working conditions of the personnel. . . . Workers . . . enjoy a higher status and gain in self-respect. Almost always, an increase in work efficiency and effectiveness is one of the results.

". . . When residential centers, group homes, and schools of normal standards, sizes, and locations are available, as well as day-care centers and workshops, the parents of the retarded can choose placements according to the individual needs of the retarded person and the needs of the family. Their choice of placement can be accomplished freely and with an easier mind, rather than being an anguished and forced choice between the horrible and the impossible.

"The closer persons in the decision-making bodies of society come to the mentally retarded, the more likely they are to render decisions resulting in appropriate and efficient programs. It may be sobering to many Americans that in Sweden, programs based on normalization principles are not dreams but actual realities brought about by the decisions of 'hard-headed' penny-pinching county council appropriation committees."

As an appendix to the paper, Nirje published sections of the then-new Swedish law, which became effective on July 1, 1968. Essentially, a Bill of Rights for the retarded, the law requires that any special treatment, training, or facilities needed by the retarded for their personal needs must be furnished by the community, including accommodations in private homes—that was the law.

When Nirje finished his extraordinary paper, he sent it immediately to Wolf Wolfensberger, then a member of the medical college faculty at the University of Nebraska, who was editing *Changing Patterns* with Robert B. Kugel. (Wolfensberger received his doctorate at Peabody Teachers College in Nashville, one of the first schools to receive federal money to study mental retardation and also the first to receive a Kennedy Foundation grant setting up a Ph.D. program in mental retardation.)

"I had heard Nirje speak, and thought what he was saying was interesting, but it didn't make a real impact on me. Then when I started to edit his paper, it was like a flash of light. This was it! The [unifying] principle that tied together much of the thinking we had all been doing! We had the beginning phrases, we called it 'humanism,' but 'the normalization principle'—here was a way of spelling it out!"

Wolfensberger had written two papers for *Changing Patterns*. One of them traced the evolution and development of residential facilities for the retarded in this country.

In that article, Wolfensberger discussed seven ways in which a retarded person has traditionally been perceived: as a sick person, a subhuman organism, a menace, an object of pity, a holy innocent, a burden of charity, and as a developing person. With the normalization principle, Wolfensberger said he realized that a framework now existed in which to enhance the possibilities for retarded individuals as developing people. He set to work on a textbook. (Wolfensberger's other article had dealt with concepts of services and management of care for retarded citizens.)

It is quite an irony that the normalization principle was then so new that Nirje's historic article, written in 1968 and published in 1969, was not translated or published in the Scandinavian countries until 1970.

The concept of "normalization" has aroused much controversy and confusion. There are people who fear for the safety of the retarded if "they" are permitted to live in the general community, and there are people who believe that "normalization" means making retarded people into "normal" people. What the term does mean is that the patterns and conditions of everyday life should be made available to the retarded so that they may live in a way that is as close to a normal lifestyle as possible. Bank-Mikkelsen, who developed the concept with Nirje, said he is sorry he ever used the word "normalization" because it has caused such misunderstanding.

"If I had it to do over again, I think I would choose a phrase like the 'principle of equality' or the 'principle of equalization.' It's the same idea, but there is less confusion about what the words mean. What is normal? Who is normal? There is so much argument about that. But equalization is a pretty clear idea, though the words mean the same thing."

"A retarded child doesn't have to become a retarded adult, if he's lucky like me, and has a job. I work hard, so I can become more like normal people," Roger said. "I don't like it when people say bad things to me."

While Nirje's article was being written, my mother consulted a vice-principal at one of the schools that Roger had attended. Although she did not know about the work then going on in Scandinavia, or about the publications of the President's Committee on Mental Retardation, or even about the National Association for Retarded Children, she was hopeful that in the years since she had last checked with the authorities in the field, something new might have developed.

The man told her to warehouse Roger.

"That got me so mad, I just can't tell you. After all of my work with him, all of our efforts to teach him to read, to groom himself and be sociable, to be told to send Roger to one of those places where he'd be ignored or harassed or sexually abused—never! I would never do that. Never!"

By coincidence, Bank-Mikkelsen himself had recently visited Sonoma (California) State Hospital, one of the state-run places Roger might have gone to had our parents taken the standard advice. His impressions were reported by the San

Francisco *Chronicle* on November 3, 1967: "In our country we would not be allowed to treat cattle like that. Perhaps you cannot treat cattle this way in your country either—cattle, after all, are useful, while the retarded are not."

Bank-Mikkelsen said Sonoma "was worse than any institution I have seen in visits to a dozen countries . . . the adults we saw, in such neglected crowds! Fifty women, living on a bare, cement floor; the smell was indescribable; ten women were naked. In another room ninety men wandered in and out of toilets without doors or partitions. The toilet room is open, adjoining a dining room where the men eat. . . . Your politicians should ask themselves, 'Would I want to live in such a hospital, or would I want my child to live there?' "

California Governor Ronald Reagan initially said that Bank-Mikkelsen's tour had been rigged by the unionized state hospital employees as a protest against Reagan's proposed reduction in their ranks. Reagan later apologized for the remark. News reports within the year claimed that conditions at Sonoma State Hospital had been improved.

I remember reading of that fight. My response was to shake my head. My mother remembers reading of it, too, and her response was to try to form her own residential facility for the retarded, which included her son.

"Why not? There was nothing else available.

"I started by talking to the business people I met through work, trying to find which ones had extra cash on hand for a tax-deductible investment. I found out about new federal money then being funneled into the state for use in facilities for the retarded. Why, this could be used at my school, I told myself," she said.

She began clipping newspaper articles on the subject and, simultaneously, began talking to the motion picture and television executives she met in her public-relations-oriented job, telling them that even if they could not "participate" in her new venture, then, at least, they might devote some air time to the subject of the mentally retarded, especially her younger son, who wrote poetry. Some of them later did.

Each Wednesday, she went to have her hair washed and set

at a beauty parlor. There, with a blue or beige protective sheet pulled up over her, she talked and talked and talked about her dream, her Search, as she called it, her desire to find a residential facility for her son, or build one, or something. The women near her nodded and smiled, before going back to the pages of their glossy magazines.

For some reason that she does not recall now, she did not have her regular Wednesday appointment one particular week in the fall of 1969. Instead, she went to the beauty parlor three days later. As she was paying her bill, the hairdresser suddenly said, "Oh, Roz! This is a person you should meet. She's involved with a group that raises money for a home for retarded children."

Standing next to my mother was another woman, also waiting to pay her bill. "I introduced myself and told her about Roger and that because there were no residential facilities for him around, I was going to build one myself."

The woman said she thought that was very nice, but before our mother did that, perhaps she would like to meet some people the woman would be with that evening: They were a group of people who raised money for a nonprofit residential facility in California, a place that had opened a few years ago. In a few hours the group would hold its annual fund-raising ball. Would Roz like to come?

"I couldn't believe what I was hearing," our mother said. "It was too good to be true."

The name of the group was CAMEO, Children's Aid, Mental, Exceptional Organization. Each year it raises about ten thousand dollars for the private nonprofit facility. Its fund-raising ball, a black-tie affair, was being held in the grand ballroom of the Beverly Hills Hotel, a palace of pink stucco set amid towering Queen palm trees on Sunset Boulevard. That evening, my mother talked her way inside the ballroom, found out who the director of the facility was, and addressed him without hesitation.

"I told him I had a retarded son and that I was trying to find him a place to live or to build one myself. I said my husband was also interested in the field of the retarded and that if we decided to send Roger to their facility, we would be active parents, helping the place to succeed."

The startled director, William T. Gray, composed himself long enough to invite the woman to the facility for a look around.

"I remember thinking, why not go? We've been disappointed so many times before, once more can't hurt," my father said.

"There's always hope, always room for a human being to develop and grow. I knew if we looked long enough and hard enough, we could prove that. An institution, wherever it was, with its flies and filth and perversion, I could never for a moment consider that for Roger. I couldn't have lived with myself if I had," Roslyn Meyers said. "I could barely live with myself as it was."

The following week they went and liked what they saw.

"The place was clean; it was well-ordered; the staff seemed to care. The way they followed Bill Gray around—I know this sounds crazy—it was like they were following Jesus. I felt Roger could be happy there," she said.

Ironically, although Roger was labeled as "retarded," he almost wasn't retarded enough to qualify for admission.

According to Sue Rehm, who was then the admissions director, "I was afraid Roger was too bright to come here, that he would actually regress if we admitted him. I had serious doubts that this would be the best place for him."

However, after conversations with my parents and Roger, the admission was approved. For the next several years, my parents continued to pay all or part of the $239 monthly fee. As the fees for the facility increased, additional aid for the "disabled" was sometimes—but not always—made available to them from the state of California.

On March 31, 1970, Roger moved, reluctantly, hesitantly, and somewhat tearfully to the residential facility.

"I told him it would be a new life, that he would have friends and a chance to live his own life," our mother said.

Our parents thought this would be the place where Roger would live for the rest of his life. However, because of the maturity he developed and because of the help he received, he lived there for only six years before moving to an apartment of his own in the community, and then welcoming to it his bride.

Several weeks after Roger moved to his new home, I was married. With both of her sons now "settled," our mother could turn her attention to the symptoms of the stress that had troubled and pained her for so long.

On April 19, 1970, the day after my wedding, Mother went down to a local church and joined Alcoholics Anonymous. Her last drink was a glass of champagne at my wedding reception.

 **11**

MIRROR

The mirror that I see There are so many
things to see lots of things make sounds
of fairies flying around with sounds of wings.
They like to sing the song of fairy love.

I can also see fireflies in the dark
Flashing their light so bright lightning bugs
are looking at my mirror in the dark
but was I there in the dark when I saw these
Flashing bugs? Yes I was, I saw there reflection
in my mirror in the dark.

We can put a picture in our mind and reflect it
on the mirror, pretending its there through the
    atmosphere
of air like in a picture of drinking wine through
    my mind
looking at my mirror.

—ROGER MEYERS

On Thursday, December 1, 1955 a bus pulled up in front of the Empire Theatre in Montgomery, Alabama. Its folding doors wheezed open and Rosa Louise Parks climbed on board, paid her ten-cent fare, and broke the law when she sat down in front.

With the action of a black woman sitting in the "whites only" section of the segregated bus, the most visible part of the American civil rights movement was launched. In its wake, a decade later, came direct challenges on behalf of mentally retarded people for decent treatment, aid, and civil rights.

"It was the times," said Bruce Ennis, legal director of the American Civil Liberties Union (ACLU). "Theories were developing of using the courts as levers of social change."

The progress Roger and Virginia have made and the services that have become available to them are also products of the times: the civil rights movement, the growth of social concern, a lessening of stigmas surrounding handicapped people, and the advent of consumerism.

In 1954, the U.S. Supreme Court held, in its historic finding in Brown vs. the Board of Education, that school children in "separate but equal" facilities were in fact being denied a full education, something they needed for complete citizenship. The court ordered the desegregation of the Topeka, Kansas, school system, and the ripples from that pebble are still being felt in communities all across the country.

The idea had been established: Persons or groups who felt cheated out of their inherent or constitutional rights by social custom or tradition could petition the courts for redress.

During the next decade, while the National Association for Retarded Citizens was gaining members around the country, while the assembled knowledge found in the book *Mental Subnormality* was being digested by the medical and scientific communities, while Representative John E. Fogarty was asking his "Fogarty questions" on Capitol Hill, while President Kennedy's Panel on Mental Retardation was preparing its report and sending its task forces around the world to learn about activities elsewhere, another grassroots movement was taking place.

At first it didn't have a name, but today we would call it "consumerism." At its core is the idea that people ought to get what they pay for, and if they don't, then they, too, can seek redress.

The public tip of this iceberg came in 1966, with the publication of Ralph Nader's book, *Unsafe at Any Speed*. Nader documented safety defects in the Corvair, a General Motors car whose structural problems caused it to be involved in an extraordinarily high number of accidents. Nader then investigated a lack of governmental and institutional concern in other matters of public health and worker safety. In 1968, he issued a scathing report on the Federal Trade Commission, the first of several systematic analyses of public institutions. In 1970, Nader established the Public Interest Research Group to pursue this avenue of investigation, and in 1971 he set up the nonprofit, tax-exempt Public Citizen organization, which was supported entirely by small donations from the public.

The legal profession, like the medical profession, had been slow to recognize the rights of millions of American citizens, and in its periodic disregard of those rights, had been negligent in its duties. But as the concept of outsiders taking a look at public and private institutions began taking hold, large foundations began contributing good chunks of money to support public-interest law firms and legal centers. Their clients would be citizens and groups who couldn't otherwise afford such broad-scale legal research and counsel. Groups such as women, Mexican-Americans, blacks, American Indians, and the handicapped—all were now able to speak with loud and clear representation.

"Lawyers are capitalists, they respond to whoever pays them," said Robert Plotkin, a senior attorney with the Mental Health Law Project, and a legal consultant to the Kennedy Foundation. "When lawyers are paid by parents, guardians, or state governments, they respond to their wishes. The traditional adversary procedure, in which there is supposed to be a balance between both sides, so that justice will prevail, just doesn't apply here, because usually no one represents the mentally retarded."

In the field of mental retardation and mental health, two of the most active legal-aid organizations have been the Public Interest Law Center of Philadelphia (PILCOP) and the Mental Health Law Project (MHLP) of Washington, D.C.

Beginning in 1972, separate court decisions established specific rights for the retarded that for generations had been denied to them: the right to education, treatment, due process in commitment proceedings, the right to be free from institutional peonage, the right to produce children, and the right to be free from harm:

• *Pennsylvania Association for Retarded Citizens vs. Commonwealth of Pennsylvania (1972).* The first major legal victory, a suit which turned into a consent decree when the state agreed that the fourteen retarded plaintiffs had been systematically denied an education equal to that of nonretarded children. Additionally, because labeling a child as "mentally retarded" imposes a serious stigma upon the child, extensive due-process procedures were demanded before the label could be imposed. "All mentally retarded persons are capable of benefiting from a program of education and training," the court wrote. "Whether [it is] begun early or not . . . a mentally retarded person can benefit at any point in his life and develop from a program of education."

- *Mills vs. Board of Education (1972).* Filed in U.S. District Court in Washington, D.C., Judge Joseph C. Waddy's decision held that all handicapped people, including the retarded, were being denied their right to an appropriate education and ordered that this be corrected.

- *Wyatt vs. Stickney (1972).* This Alabama case established that retarded people had the right to developmental and ameliorative treatment in the least restrictive environment, that they had the right to individualized treatment programs, a humane physical and psychological environment, and an adequate and qualified staff.

- *Jackson vs. Indiana (1972).* The U.S. Supreme Court held that it was a denial of equal protection and due process to confine a mentally retarded person until he should become "competent." Prior to the ruling, the M'Naghten Rule of "innocent by reason of insanity" was often applied to retarded people, a ruling that confused mental illness and mental retardation. Under M'Naghten, a retarded person accused of a crime could not be tried until he had been found "competent," or not retarded. That meant he was usually confined to a mental hospital for what was, in effect, a life sentence. In this case, the Supreme Court held that within a reasonable time after a person is incarcerated, the state must either release him or go through a civil procedure to have him committed. Additionally, the nature and duration of commitment "must" bear some reasonable relation to the purpose for which the individual has been committed.

- *Souder vs. Brennan (1973)* established that the retarded in institutions must not be subject to involuntary peonage through low wages, and mandated that the federal Department of Labor must enforce provisions of the 1966 Fair Labor Standards Act for people within institutions.
- *Wyatt vs. Aderholt (1974).* A federal court in Alabama upheld the right of the retarded person to procreate and declared unconstitutional the applicable Alabama law permitting easy resort to compulsory sterilization.
- *New York State Association for Retarded Citizens, et al. vs. State of New York (1975).* This case concerned the institution on Staten Island known as Willowbrook. It also resulted in a consent decree decision establishing that retarded people in institutions have the right to be free from harm (which could either be physical abuse or poor nutrition). It also stated that retarded people have the right to improve themselves, which means teaching and training procedures must be set up for them.

One issue for which there is as yet no firm decision is the question of who best represents the interests of the retarded person? For example, when the subject of commitment to a public or private facility comes up, do parents or guardians automatically represent the best interests of their charge, or should the retarded person who is about to be placed there be represented by legal counsel of his own? Such a concept might place the attorneys for the retarded person at loggerheads with the attorneys for the parents or guardians, but if a retarded individual is an individual who cannot speak for himself, shouldn't an attorney do it for him? Ultimately, the Supreme Court may have to decide.

The severely wounded soldiers of World War I were known as basket cases and left to live on pallets. The severely wounded soldiers of World War II were known as rehabilitation patients, their fractured arms and legs exercised, stimulated, and sometimes replaced, and they drive down streets in specially equipped cars, able to live as normal people.

In World War II, prisoner-of-war camp soldiers were tortured and brainwashed; back home many of them were restored to much of their former mental health.

"Historically it took the horrors of World War II before work in mental retardation could go forward," said Gunnar Dybwad, Professor Emeritus of Human Development at Brandeis University. "During the war, we learned you could break any individual under stress, but we also learned you could mend an individual as well."

Dybwad is a major figure in the field of mental retardation. He is an attorney and criminologist who has been executive director of the National Association for Retarded Citizens (1957 to 1963), and head of an international mental-retardation project headquartered in Geneva, Switzerland (1963 to 1967).

His wife, Rosemary Dybwad, is also an important researcher with an international scholarship created in her honor.

Gunnar Dybwad says, "Mental retardation as a cultural phenomenon shows up in similar patterns around the world, and yet after World War II there was a sudden flareup of interest in it. Why? There was no discernible cause, no great world leader in the field, no single book or conference. Yet things began happening in the late 1940s and 1950s in the Scandinavian countries, in America, England, Belgium, and elsewhere. Why? Perhaps because by comparison with what we had seen in the war, we started putting greater value on human life, on human rights, began applying the rehabilitation processes we had learned in the war to the mentally retarded. There was the G.I. bill and the baby boom and emphasis on education—but if you have more babies, you also have more mentally-retarded babies, and so the parent groups got going. If we could mend the war-injured, we could mend others too."

For the historic 1969 publication *Changing Patterns in Resident Services for the Mentally Retarded*, it was Dybwad who was called on to write the important "Overview" chapter, which summarized the discussion papers and pointed out possible future developments.

"The concept of the mentally retarded person as a *person* is very new, not stated anywhere until just a few years ago. 'Holy

Roger and his mother in 1954.

Robert Meyers in the newsroom of the Washington *Post. Photo by Linda Wheeler.*

Virginia as Rose Queen at the Woods Schools.

Waiting: best man and groom before the wedding. *Photo by Larry Armstrong.*

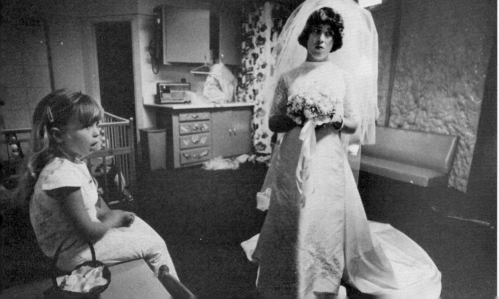

The wedding. *Photo by Larry Armstrong.*

Waiting: flower girl Jana Schneider and
bride-to-be before the wedding. *Photo
by Larry Armstrong.*

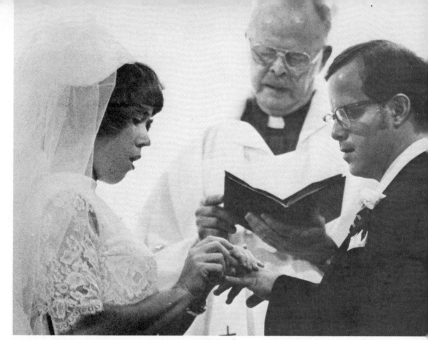

The ring. Virginia, the Reverend Edwin A. Svendsen, Roger. *Photo by Larry Armstrong.*

At the wedding reception, counselor Carol Knieff talks with Roger and Virginia. *Photo by Larry Armstrong.*

Cutting the cake. Flower girl Jana Schneider, Roger, Virginia. *Photo by Larry Armstrong.*

Roger and Virginia at their kitchen table, pasting trading stamps in books as a cost-cutting measure.
Photo by Larry Armstrong.

Roger reads the daily paper while Virginia works on the trading stamps.
Photo by Larry Armstrong.

Roger works on his math at home. He believes that in twenty or thirty years he will know enough to become a schoolteacher. *Photo by Larry Armstrong.*

Roger on the job.
Photos by Larry Armstrong.

Roger in the middle of it all. *Photo by Larry Armstrong.*

Roger and waitress Toni Frazier during a break in work. *Photo by Larry Armstrong.*

"San Francisco." Roger copied a photograph of a San Francisco scene, then colored it with crayons, mainly browns and greens. It hangs, framed, in the Meyers' kitchen. *Photo by Larry Armstrong.*

Virginia and Roger Meyers. *Photo by Larry Armstrong.*

Innocents,' as the Catholic Church called them; 'eternal Children,' the title of a film by the Canadian Film Board; those books, *The Child Who Never Grew* [by Pearl S. Buck] and *Angel Unaware* [Dale Evans Rogers]—these are the titles of objects, not people," Dybwad said.

"Mental retardation is in many ways a social problem. We have some people who need some help. If we let the label 'mentally retarded' stand in the way of delivering that help, we have libeled these people. We have to deliver those services to the home where the mother can help her child, to the school, where retardation is often first spotted, to the community later on. The jargon that the educators developed—that some retarded persons are 'educable,' while some are only 'trainable'—is intellectual sleight-of-hand. All persons can learn," he said.

In 1921, while sitting on a hillside overlooking Geneva, Switzerland, an Englishwoman named Eglantyne Jebb wrote out what she called a "Declaration of the Rights of the Child," the first such document of its kind; it made no specific mention of mental retardation, however.

Jebb's document was adopted by the League of Nations, but forgotten after the League collapsed. The United Nations issued its own statement on the rights of children in 1959, but it too ignored the mentally retarded.

The national parents' movements of the 1950s, including those in the United States and the Scandinavian countries, soon led to the formation of an international society to coordinate their information and interests. In 1967, the International League of Societies for the Mentally Handicapped passed its own resolution on the individual rights of the mentally retarded.

"That was something, *individual* rights, but still no mention of people," Dybwad said.

That was changed, for the first time in 1971, when the United Nations General Assembly adopted the statement with minor changes. One major change was in the title, however: It now referred to the rights of mentally retarded *persons*.

"I don't know what genius thought of this, but he must have known what he was doing," Dybwad said.

While it is unclear what significance the United Nations

declaration has on such things as state funding for early intervention programs, or the training of counselors for the field, or public acceptance of community group homes, it did, for the first time, according to Gunnar Dybwad, "express world-wide recognition of the dignity of man no matter how limited or handicapped he is."

In 1972, Wolf Wolfensberger, by then a visiting scholar with the National Institute on Mental Retardation in Toronto, Canada, wrote *Normalization (The Principle of Normalization in Human Services)*. Drawing on his previous work, some of it in the 1969 volume entitled *Changing Patterns in Residential Services for the Mentally Retarded*, Wolfensberger described the development of the normalization principle in Scandinavia, giving credit to Bank-Mikkelsen and Nirje.

When *Mental Subnormality* had been published in 1958, it had been the first comprehensive look at mental retardation in all its various medical and social aspects. Now, only fourteen years later, another comprehensive book articulating humane methods and attitudes concerning mental retardation had been created. Between the covers of the book were major essays covering education, counseling, training, guidance, residential facilities, and the support of retarded people, along with specific examples of the successful application of these principles, mainly in Scandinavia. The book brought together much of the work that had been done by so many others on the local, state, and federal levels. Its essays referred back to historical events; its writers showed how the past influenced the present; its attitudes looked to the future. *Normalization* became widely used as a textbook in college and university classes and as a reference work for people in the field. It was on the shelves of every single professional I interviewed.

Additionally, Wolfensberger devised a system of objectively measuring whether money was being spent on services for the retarded, as it would be by people following the normalization principle, or if public funds were only being spent to warehouse and coddle the retarded, as they would be under the traditional "protectionist" approach to the field.

Wolfensberger called the scale the Program Analysis of Service Systems (PASS). It is comprised of forty-one specific points on which a facility can be graded. The forty-one points include such matters as whether the retarded people are living in warehouses, in hospital beds, or whether the individual lives in clean, pleasant surroundings, with privacy, in an atmosphere that approximates as much as possible a home-style environment; whether the attitude of the counselors is patronizing or condescending toward them; or whether the individual is addressed with respect and dignity; and so on. (The PASS scale has since been adopted in whole or in part by the states of Pennsylvania, Nebraska, and California.)

"It is knowing, *knowing* what can be done, and doing it, that is important. It is being a witness to the truth that counts," Wolfensberger said.

"Any number of Judeo-Christian precepts are constructively relevant to our society and to the handicapped people within it—the sacredness of life, mutual support, and enabling others to live as both a duty and a privilege. Maimonides's idea of charity, or of real personal Christian charity, *demands* contact with the poor and suffering. So if we know what to do, how can we do anything less?"

Wolfensberger's emotional statements make him a controversial figure. His own feeling is that his values come from the facts he has studied, and that the facts merit his emotional response. Additionally, the fact that he has taken an advocacy position on the issues, which puts him at odds with traditional academic thinking, doesn't bother him. "A scholar is (traditionally) not supposed to advocate. . . . But look at what the retarded suffer. There is bodily damage, functional loss, rejection by parents and society, segregation, status degradation, involuntary poverty, impoverishment of experience, loss of autonomy, of control, and of their own freedom. Just think what it does to a retarded person to know he is the source of anguish to those who love him—and the handicapped person *knows* he has caused anguish, so he feels bad, evil, and worthless for having been the cause of someone else's suffering."

"The retarded person is seen by others and himself as being deviant, not just different from others, but as being less than others, less of a person, less of a human being. Normalization is deviancy-unmaking. It tries to remediate the wound, the physical wound—for example, brain damage—through rehabilitation and training. This way we can remediate the functional loss, the ability of the retarded person to function in society. But deviancy is also in the eye of the beholder, and, therefore, we try to use images for the retarded that are normalized."

In the PASS seminars, for example, Wolfensberger and his student assistants spend, literally, hours going over the conceptual manner in which the retarded are viewed by others: the adults who are called children, the impoverished residential facilities with poetic names involving happy acres, farms, and pleasant valleys; the segregation of sexes in institutions that, not surprisingly, often leads to homosexuality—an imposed condition for which the retarded are then devalued even further; the "language of architecture" in which windows are barred so the retarded won't "hurt" themselves; the location of the facility miles from the nearest community; the enormous size of the facility so that the retarded get no more than minimal care, not training and guidance, the menial jobs they are given (not the productive jobs they choose); the denials of their freedoms, rights, sense of self, and humanness.

In the broadest sense, Wolfensberger said, "Normalization tries to reintroduce traditional values to our dealing with the retarded, tries to reintroduce real charity, kindness, and concern. It is not so much that we exercise our freedom by doing that, but that we help others to lead their own lives as independently as they can."

He said, however, that this is only part of an historical process. "The literature has not been honest about work in the field. The retarded were often destroyed—*destroyed*—in institutions; these were not places of considerate care. They would be hosed down in rooms with open windows, so they caught pneumonia and died. Rarely has this been written up. But even when that was exposed, it was replaced only by a system of neglect: put the retarded way far away, so they won't be seen and will be comfortable—that's what the theory was. . . . So what we are talking about [now] is the traditional and direct charity and love to others. If we can see the good way to go, if we can develop an approach to helping the retarded achieve their full potential, to live with us as our brothers and sisters and friends and neighbors, then we must go that way. It is the act that is important, not whether we succeed at all or all the time, but the act, not the end, but the act."

In 1950, when the National Association for Retarded Citizens was formed, there was so little money spent on the local, state, and federal levels for the benefit of the retarded that no one bothered to keep count. Today the federal government spends more than $2.7 billion in the field, and state and local governments budget more than $3.3 billion, according to Fred J. Krause, executive director of the President's Committee on Mental Retardation.

On October 30, 1970, President Richard Nixon signed the Developmental Disabilities Act, an umbrella concept urged by NARC, United Cerebral Palsy, Inc., the Council for Exceptional Children, and several professional groups. The cumbersome term was chosen after furious debate in an attempt to lessen some of the bloodletting that had frequently gone on among special-interest groups competing for the federal dollar, and to specifically define the field in such a way as to differentiate it from mental health. The concept of the legislation was to provide the states with more flexibility in providing services to a wider variety of people, with less reliance on rigid medical criteria.

On November 16, 1971, President Nixon launched what has become known as the "deinstitutionalization policy," committing the federal government to drastically reducing the number of people housed in state institutions. In 1971, when the issue was stated, there were approximately 190,000 to 200,000 people in institutions. In 1978, the number was about 170,000 and is expected to drop to about 130,000 by 1980.

Persons leaving institutions are going into a wide variety of alternative-placement centers, including group homes, foster homes, boarding facilities, intermediate-care facilities (where they can learn how to live independently or semi-independently), and so on. These living arrangements are, in theory, more humane environments for retarded individuals than institutions.

Of course, former institution residents are not the only ones going into these alternative placements. There are many persons who go there after living with their parents or in private facilities.

According to Paul Marchand, head of the Washington office of NARC, the following are other significant pieces of federal legislation.

• Intermediate Care Facilities for the Mentally Retarded. Passed in 1972 as part of the Medicaid legislation, it provides reimbursements to the states for group home-type settings.

• The 1973 Rehabilitation Act provides vocational training for adults.

• The Supplemental Security Income (SSI) program, passed in 1974, provides money in direct cash benefits to qualified disabled persons, including the retarded.

• Housing and loan assistance, passed in 1974, provides money for housing.

• The 1975 Social Services Program authorized services to the retarded.

• The 1975 Education for All Handicapped Children Act demands that "free, appropriate" public education for all children between the ages of five and eighteen be in effect by 1978.

This last piece of legislation is regarded by authorities as possibly the most important piece of legislation ever passed on behalf of retarded persons. By making it federal policy that all handicapped people receive a free, appropriate education, the legislation goes a long way toward eliminating the fear and frustration faced by Roger, Virginia, and their parents: How will our children learn, if we cannot afford the money to educate them? This legislation was in part the result of the PARC vs. Pennsylvania consent decree, and the Mills vs. Board of Education decision. Both were resolved in 1972, and both found that retarded children were not receiving adequate educations. Additionally, the act, known as Public Law 94-142, includes help for so many children with a wide range of disabilities (for example, learning problems and deafness) that fully 12 percent of all school children could receive help under its intent.

The development of the civil rights movement, the opening of public-interest law firms, and an awareness of the rights of retarded persons have all served to equalize the balance somewhat. But it is still a very long uphill battle until there is equal justice for all.

 **12**

REFLECTION

It has been going on for so many years.
Reflection. The image that stays through light
Sometimes it goes away at night, but not always.
But reflection is there. Through the
Atmosphere of air from the sun's
Rays of light. God made us big and bright
If we look at our selfs in each others eyes
We see each others image. We love each other.
Love is to share, love is everywhere

Do you know that I can reflect your love
From my love of image, cause I care so much
About you. And I know you reflect my love from
Your love of image.

When it's dark at night we can still see
Our reflection by moonlight or by turning
On our flashlight. But if there's no moonlight
No flashlight no light at all, Our reflection
Would be nothing unless we look at our selfs.

Through a puddle of rainwater with very sharp eyes,
If we stand in the rain for a very long time,
Our image looks like its crying, by rain drops hitting
The water making ripple rings around our necks
Or like we are crying with teardrops falling down hitting
Something like our desk, so many teardrops make
A puddle and seeing our image of how sad sorry or lonely
We are.

If you go away from me you look small,
Like a small standing doll in front of a mirror.
But when you come back to stay with me I want to say
Your love is with me always. I can picture you in
My mind the image of you the likeness of you.
You're so beautifully made by God
That your love will always stay with me, forever.

—ROGER MEYERS

Shortly after Roger arrived at his new home, his schoolbooks and records packed in brown cardboard boxes, his multicolored Hoola-hoops stacked against the wall, and still worried about whether "the teachers are strict and if the kids are rough," he spotted two things that intrigued him.

The first was a balloon in the shape of a rabbit, which had been covered with papier-maché, painted white, and with a pretty mouth painted on with red lipstick. The artist later explained, "It started out to be Bugs Bunny, but I knew that Bugsy wasn't married yet, so I called it Mrs. Bugs Bunny."

The second was a shy young girl with soft brown hair who seemed to know a great deal about the facility, and often took charge of feeding the younger residents. In fact, it can now be reliably reported that the newcomer and the old-timer eyed each other for several days, sizing each other up without saying a word.

Then one day, Roger asked his housemother who had made the rabbit display. The woman pointed to the shy young girl with the soft brown hair and said that her name was Virginia Rae Hensler.

"We met at the bunny rabbit," Roger likes to say. "And ever since then I've called her my bunny."

Every time he says this, Virginia, who likes to hear a good story retold as much as anyone, laughs in delight.

Lost to history are their first words to each other, although each believes it was nothing more than an exchange of names and pertinent information. Virginia, who by 1970 had lived at the facility for three years, offered to show Roger the ropes. He accepted.

"Roger was gregarious, and had an ability to get around and make friends, but he seemed to withdraw when there weren't enough challenges for him," Bill Gray, the facility's former director, remembers.

Parents of retarded children and adults who are placed in the care of others face the question: Is there enough for them to do? Are there activities and are they worthwhile, or is it all only make-work? Do these activities teach the retarded how to live in the society at large, or are they only to make the parents feel better?

Initially, there was not enough for Roger to do. Among his earliest "jobs" was yard work, a task that did little to challenge him. When work was over, he would retreat to his room (sometimes he had a roommate, though he preferred living alone), writing his poetry or listening to his record collection.

"One day I was showing some people around, and Roger came out of his room," recalled Sue Rehm, a former social worker at the facility. "I introduced Roger to the people, and, as soon as I did, he went back to his room and came back doing his Hoola-hoop routine. I thought to myself, 'My God! Have we done this to him? That someone with all his potential is reduced to showing off his Hoola-hoop skills to strangers?' "

Once Roger was established at the facility, a new and particularly twentieth-century role-reversal change came over our family. In the past, it was our mother who handled the responsibility (which was sometimes a burden, sometimes a chore) of taking Roger from doctor to doctor, from counseling center to rehabilitation agency, of talking about building her own home for the retarded when she could find nothing suitable, of making sure he was placed in the one she finally discovered through the casual conversation in a beauty shop.

But with Roger established at the facility, my father took over as his essential family support, answering his long-distance telephone questions, buying him a needed pair of pants, getting his shoes reheeled, taking him into the community. He did this at least twice a month, sometimes once a week, driving the 135 miles from his home to Roger's in the morning, and then driving the return 135 miles, sometimes on the same day.

"I had a feeling of remorse that I hadn't spent more time with him when he was an infant. But there always seemed to be the press of business. Once we knew he was retarded, I had this desire to get some equity, so that when I left this world I would leave something behind for him," he said.

With Roger at the facility, he found out about a parents' group whose members also had retarded offspring at the facility. It was the first time, he said, that he had actually discovered a group of people with interests in this area similar to his own. He joined the group, and one year later became its president.

The state of California had by then established a regional center system as the vehicle to provide services to the retarded. The state was divided into regions, and the retarded individual was "registered" with one of them. Roger for a time was registered with the L.A. regional center, the division headed by Richard Koch, M.D.

The parents' group to which our father belonged often used an auditorium at the L.A. regional center Children's Hospital in which the L.A. regional center division was located, and where Koch was director of the Child Development Division. The two men struck up an acquaintance. Bob Meyers.told Koch, "The regional center system is the best-kept secret in California." He offered to write free promotional advertising copy for the system, an offer that Koch accepted. Later, in semi-retirement, he was paid $6,000 annually as a consultant to Children's Hospital in matters of public information on services to the retarded.

Such services are still among the best-kept secrets in California and across the country. After the newspaper series appeared, I received requests for information from people around the country, wanting to know where they could go for help. One of the calls was from a well-known television personality in Los Angeles. He had an adult retarded son, but didn't feel the counselors he had talked with had given him all the information available on the subject. The man had never heard of the regional center system. I gave him the address. It is located about a mile from his office.

Often when our father visited Roger, he would be surrounded as soon as he entered the facility by a dozen retarded persons. "They were lonely," he said. "Some of the kids hadn't seen their families in years. Some of the adults had never had a visitor. Can you imagine that? I didn't want Roger to think he'd been rejected." He shrugged. "Love makes the world go round."

Once Roger's bags were unpacked at the facility, he became a part of the developing social system of compassionate services for the retarded. He was no longer seen against a background of neurological tests and slow-bone-development scales, but against a foreground of vocational training, budget management, personal grooming skills, the triumph of taking a bus, and the victory of choosing what to do with his life. Not all at once, and some of it not even today, but he and Virginia were in a position to benefit from work in the field, from the normalization principle from Scandinavia, from the lawsuits that had been and would be filed around this country, from the attempts to change attitudes about the retarded from pity or fear to attitudes that accepted the retarded as people, and from workers who set out to help them lead lives that would be as independent as possible.

"I'll never forget sitting down to dinner with your parents one night, and telling them again and again that the facility was not a permanent residence for Roger, that it was only one stage for him," said Bill Gray. "I didn't see it as a place that would shelter him for the rest of his life, but only as a place that would help him learn as much as he could."

Gray's words are an unconscious echo of the thoughts expressed by Samuel Gridley Howe more than a century earlier—that with temporary help and education in small facilities, the retarded could be returned to fruitful lives in their communities. So much had intervened since Howe set forth his theory.

But the idea that Roger might soon be moving out into the community, away from their protecting wing, was (and is) a difficult idea for our parents to absorb. After all, they had spent more than twenty years trying to find the right facility for him. Now that they had finally found such a place, they were hearing that it was not the final answer.

"Sometimes change can come at you very quickly," our father sighed.

"We tend to put our fears onto the retarded. They know what they can do, but because they trust us and depend on us, they get confused when we say we're not sure of their abilities," said Pastor Ed Svendsen.

In the early 1970s, Bill Gray and other administrators at the home were able to work out programs and classes for their retarded residents at a number of the local schools, classes which never existed before. The significance for Roger and Virginia was that with half the facility's 150 or so persons attending classes elsewhere during the day, the remaining counselors and guidance personnel could work more closely with them.

Suddenly, rather than having television as their only contact with life outside the facility, Roger was making scheduled trips to the local park, to shopping centers, to movies, and to bowling matches. There were outings to local restaurants, which entailed the necessity of being able to read, so that you could understand the menu, and the ability to choose new dishes to eat. He had to figure out which coins would pay for what dish, and remember to leave a tip. Roger had to learn to wait his turn in line, and to knock off the mannerisms and gestures that "everyone" used at the facility—because this was a real restaurant and you would be accepted or not based on your own behavior.

"It was a chance for eyeryone to get out and see what the real world was like," Bill Gray said.

Roger and Virginia were hanging around together a great deal. A relationship of friendship and brother-and-sister feelings gradually developed into one of need and dependence. Roger, who fancied himself a Lothario, liked to play his records for other girls in the facility, and Virginia decided this would be all right if he put his arm only around her when they were sitting on the couch in the main living room, while watching television.

Once he put his arm around another girl, and there was such hell to pay that they didn't talk to each other for weeks.

Virginia sometimes read his poems, "and I made sure he dotted his i's and crossed his t's. We would help each other. When he jiggled his leg, I would put my hand on it and say, 'Stop it, honey. You're making me nervous.' "

When the facility built a swimming pool, Roger went for half-hour swims at 4 P.M. each day, although Virginia, deathly afraid of the water because someone had once pushed her in at the Woods Schools, refused.

"Then Roger came along and told me not to worry, that I

wouldn't sink because God was holding me up," she said. She now swims.

One day they were walking on a residential street near their facility. "Suddenly a large dog jumped out at us and he started barking, really loud," Roger said.

"I was scared. I didn't know what to do and I couldn't move," Virginia related.

Not knowing what else to do, Roger started barking at the dog in return. The dog turned tail and ran.

In 1970, shortly after arriving at the facility, Roger began participating in the Special Olympics, a series of athletic events for retarded people in which no records are ever set or broken, but in which victory is achieved by participation. The Special Olympics were established in 1968 by the Kennedy Foundation, after its research showed that few retarded children or adults were getting any physical attention at all; and, worse, that many educators and coaches thought that exercise of any kind, much less competition, was beyond the "ability" of retarded people. Within the last decade the Foundation's figures show that more than one million people in the United States and twelve foreign countries have participated.

Roger used to run in the dashes, the 50-yard dash, the 220-yard dash, and the 440-yard dash, and, less frequently, he would enter the 25-yard back-stroke swim competition. In our parents' files are a dozen blue, red, and yellow ribbons for first-, second-, and third-place finishes in the regional events.

One year, however, he didn't make the team in his favored event, the 50-yard dash. It was a four-man field, and as they broke from the starting blocks and raced down the cinder track, Roger fell into third place, beyond two young men.

Suddenly, the first- and second-place leaders stopped cold. For some reason—the pressure of running, the pounding muscles, the shortness of breath—they couldn't go on.

"I stopped too. I thought they might be sick. I didn't want them to feel bad," Roger said. He put his arm around one of them, to comfort him.

The remaining entrant, the guy in fourth place, won.

Roger and Virginia were learning, taking in every piece of

information given to them and turning it to their own use. When Virginia's mother flew in to visit them, she found Roger and Virginia holding hands in the airport terminal, waiting for her with exciting news.

The news was that they now knew how to use the public bus transportation system so well that they had traveled on two different buses from their residential facility to meet her.

"They were so proud that they could do it that they wanted to prove it to me. So we all took the two buses back from the airport to the home," she said.

The trip took four hours.

"I had to pay my own way."

In classes, Virginia was working hard, very hard, to master the finer points of learning. She got the D, T, and L sounds down pat, and began work on speaking with less of a nasal whine. She would shut her eyes and listen to herself speak, and then practice the words until one of her teachers told her she was doing well.

Roger had a post as a teacher's aide at the facility, and he could often be found in the classrooms, working with people whose handicaps were greater than his. His duties involved handing out toys and teaching devices, and collecting them at the end of the day. He also tried to help his friend Lionel improve his writing.

Another person he associated with was Amy, a girl of nine or ten who was autistic; meaning that she, virtually, never responded to anyone or anything outside of herself.

Roger liked to sit and talk with Amy, who was a frail, doll-like creature with stringy brown hair. She sometimes recognized him when he came into her classroom. One day Roger helped her with one of the projects and, to thank him, she squeezed his hand. Roger rightly counts this as a triumph.

Roger was paid fifty cents a day for his work as a teachers' aide, and, as he and Virginia began making their way around the community, he began seeing ways in which he could spend more money. There were movies to go to, dinners to buy, buses to take, and books that he needed for his self-taught study program. He told the administrators that he thought he should be paid a decent wage for his job and shown respect as a classroom aide. When they refused, he said, "I quit."

"It was one of the best decisons he ever made," said Bill Stein, a psychiatric social worker who later came to play a major part in Roger and Virginia's lives when he counseled them for marriage. "It showed he had a good sense of his own self-worth. When the administrators wouldn't pay him for his work, he denied them his work. I couldn't agree more."

He showed his sense of self-worth in another way, too. As a working man, as a consumer of services, he didn't like wasting his time. His mother recalls this story: "Once when he had a dentist's appointment he waited and waited in the dentist's office, and, finally, when he had waited too long he walked out." Roger found another dentist.

One summer he went with his colleagues from the residential facility on a trip to the Flamingo Hotel in Las Vegas. "We saw a nightclub act with dancing girls, and I drank so many Manhattans I got dizzy," he said.

His restaurant job proved his worth, and got him out of the facility for hours at a time. But, in the early days, because his residential facility still represented a safe and secure world for him, when he decided he needed more money, he turned to poetry and art work as fields in which he could earn more cash, and yet not give up his secure base.

"Your parents were always praising him for these artsy-craftsy things, while I was trying to get him out on his own. He'd put his energy into these things, and so wouldn't work as hard on the other matters," Stein said.

Roger recopied all of his poems, and put them into manuscript form. Then, in an attempt to get them published, he took the traditional over-the-transom route and sent one poem, "What Mentally Retarded Means," which is reprinted at the beginning of Chapter 1, off to President Richard M. Nixon.

"Dear Mr. President, hello," states the letter, written on March 5, 1973. "I write poems. And I am sending you a poem, called 'What Mentally Retarded Means.' This poem got published before in the Methodist Church newspaper and . . . I would like for you to publish it also in your paper and I would like very much to have some kind of an award for it.

"My name is Roger Meyers. I live at [a facility] which is for the retarded and I am a teacher. I work, play, and live with the retarded [cause I am one myself] borderline average. Please write to me. . . . Sincerely yours, Roger."

President Nixon must have been busy with other matters at that time, because Roger's letter was forwarded to Fred J. Krause, Executive Director of the President's Committee on Mental Retardation.

"Dear Mr. Meyers," Krause wrote on March 26, 1973. "President Nixon has asked me to thank you for your letter concerning the publication of your poem 'What Mentally Retarded Means.'

"I appreciate the fact that you have written such a beautiful poem; however, we do not publish any materials other than those that are prepared by the staff or consultants of the President's Committee on Mental Retardation. Thank you for sharing your talent with us. With kindest regards. Sincerely yours. . . ."

When the attempt to get Presidential sponsorship of his poems failed, Roger began bugging our parents to do something about it. Our mother's eventual solution was to find two young men and convince them to publish Roger's poetry alongside sentimental pictures of little children running sprite-like through unpolluted streams in pastoral meadows. The two young men actually went down to visit Roger, and encouraged him to keep on "grinding 'em out." But when they told him they wouldn't be able to give him any money until after the book had been published, he pulled out of the deal.

Several years later, in 1975, Roger decided he would like to improve his ability at "art work." He answered an art institute ad on the inside of a matchbook cover and enrolled in its course.

After the request-for-information card was sent in, a salesman called on Roger at his residential facility and signed him up. The total cost was $695, toward which Roger was required to pay $25 down and $25 a month. For his money, he received charcoal sticks, artists' pads, tracing paper, erasers, and a portfolio in which to keep it all.

Some of the handwritten comments of the instructors were encouraging: "contours of objects very well drawn . . . I enjoyed reviewing your work!"

Others harped on things he hadn't done properly: "Grade tones from dark to light to show contrast. . . . Good drawing! Refer to lesson 2, page 21 on 'tone patterns' . . . Use contrast of tone to give these shapes volume and depth. . . ."

After about eight lessons, however (about one a month), Roger began to lose interst. There were other projects to occupy his mind, new patterns of personal development with his new counselors to work on. The lessons stopped being fun, and he stopped sending them in.

But the bills kept coming.

Now a new problem developed: He had known how to start the art project, but he didn't know how to stop it. In fact, since he had signed a contract with the company, he couldn't stop it. Dunning postcards and then a dunning letter arrived in the mail. One of the counselors found out about them and told Roger's parents.

"A salesman was called, but he said he was no longer connected with the company," our father said. "So I wrote the company a letter, and said I was 'surprised' to discover that they would sell their course on the grounds of a facility for the mentally retarded."

The threat of a lawsuit, or at least rotten publicity, riddled the letter, and the company promptly issued Roger a full refund in the amount of $236.20.

Roger has spent his hard-earned money on short-lived projects at other times, too. Once he bought a beautiful new guitar for $64, paid for his own guitar lessons, then stopped; the guitar sits in a corner of his apartment. Once he bought a building-block set and never used it. Once he spent $50 on an imported French doll, which he told his mother he "might someday" give to some little kid he knew; the doll sat in his closet.

He went down to his local Sears store one day and bought a pair of black trousers made of cotton twill. He chose the color because that is the color the manager at the restaurant makes him wear—and he could always wear those same trousers when he wasn't working.

The problem was the pants were long, way too long. He could have hoisted himself up on stilts and the pants would still have been too long. But, since he had bought them, he wore them. Bill Stein, his counselor, saw Roger walking down the hallway of the facility one day, his black pants hiked "up to his throat."

"I said, 'Roger, do you know what you look like?' Roger said he didn't so I said, 'Let me show you.' "

Another counselor, Don Simons, was walking down the hall at the same time, and Stein asked him to imitate Roger, while Roger watched.

Simons hoisted his own pants up as high as they would go, and then started waddling down the hall, imitating Roger, who was forced to waddle as he walked because the crotch of the pants was pulled so tightly into his groin.

"Roger burst out laughing. He said Don looked ridiculous. I agreed and said, 'Look, when you go out into the community, you've got two strikes against you, because you're retarded. You can't let people throw the third strike at you because you're dressed funny. You've got to try twice as hard as everybody else just to get by.' Roger said he understood."

Then Stein, still talking with Roger in the hallway, addressed the issue of the lunch pail Roger was carrying. It had characters from "Land of the Lost" painted on it. "I asked him why he was using that particular one, and he said the characters were from one of his favorite TV shows. That was a good reason, but the fact was that if he, then twenty-five years old, went into the community carrying a children's lunch bucket, people were going to think he was a big baby." One traditional perception of the retarded is that they are children who never grow.

"So Roger went back to his room, changed his pants, and found a black lunch pail which he then began using," Stein said.

When Roger's father came down to visit, a short time later, he saw the pants and hit the ceiling. "How could the counselors let him *do* such a thing? How could they let him waste his money, or wear those pants? Why didn't they have them altered?" he asked.

Stein, a tough-talking guy from the Bronx, just shrugged. "Look, I don't do trousers. I'm trying to help Roger learn how to live on his own. The only way he's going to learn is by making mistakes."

That weekend, our father drove his son back to Sears, and they exchanged the pants for a pair that fit.

The existence of the laws, legislative programs, Presidential decrees, and funding that made Roger's residence at the facility possible does not mean the end of his problems, however. Much of the money goes for research, physical structures, and other needed items which do not have an immediate impact on the individual. A bureaucratic morass has been created among federal, state, and local authorities, and competing agencies within each of those jurisdictions, which does not always work to the advantage of retarded people.

In the early 1970s, there was a change-over in the way in which funds were delivered: Some new divisions were created and some old ones restructured. Lost in the shuffle was a $114-per-month appropriation to which Roger was entitled and which was paid directly to his residential facility to cover a tuition increase.

During 1973, our parents sent letters and made phone calls to all of their elected representatives, to legislative committees, and to private consulting groups—nothing worked. By 1974, they were more than $1,600 behind in payments to the facility. They began getting veiled threats from the facility that Roger's place there would have to be "re-evaluated" if the debt were not paid.

"It was as if we were starting all over again," our mother said.

Finally, I got in touch with a state senate aide I happened to know. He made one call from his San Francisco office: "The Senator wants to know whether Roger Meyers is entitled to the additional funds, and if he is entitled, why hasn't he received them?"

Within days the Gordian knot of red tape had been slashed, and the funds were released.

But what about all the people caught in the same snare, who don't have sons or relatives who are drinking buddies with state senate aides?

The answer is, those people suffer precisely what my parents suffered through, with no guarantee of a satisfactory conclusion.

13

THE IMAGE OF BLIND PEOPLE

The image of blind people can only see
With their eye vision closed. Their mind is
Way behind, but yet the other side of their mind
is open and so that is never closing, never folding
but it's unfolding by something they see.
Something they feel like a tree, feeling the
strings of an instrument, or rain, and other
things in life

—ROGER MEYERS

"They wouldn't let us be alone together, and if we were in the same room, we had to leave the door open. It was as if they didn't trust us," Roger said, describing the difficult circumstances under which he and Virginia lived and courted while in their residential facility.

"Houseparents would criticize us if we held hands or if I put my arm around her," he said. If they kissed goodnight, they did it quickly, when no one was looking.

Their interest was affection, something few people were as yet willing to "grant" them. What they were "granted" was the right to remain in continuing adolescence, with little growth or progress.

But they knew better.

When they looked beyond the chain-link fence of their residential facility, they saw that other young couples their age, and within their own facilities, got married and went to live on their own. Although at this time they still were not able to make change, or handle themselves with real confidence in the outside community, they began talking about marriage.

"One day, I asked Virginia to marry me," Roger said. "I went down on my knee and I asked her." They had known each other less than a year.

"I said, 'Yes, but let's wait awhile, honey, until I finish the [vocational] class I'm in,'" Virginia responded.

As a sign of his fidelity, Roger took an inexpensive "pearl" they had won at an outing with Virginia's mother and had it made up as an engagement ring. Then each night they would sit together in his room at the facility, where he was not allowed to shut the door if someone else was in the room.

"Marriage was seen as a ticket out for them," recalled Don Simons, one of their counselors at the time. "I don't think either of them realized all the responsibility involved. Their desire to get married was unrealistic. Roger was motivated to earn money, but he had no concept of living on his own, of what costs were. He verbalized his wishes and fantasies to others who thought, Gee, how unrealistic he is. Then the two of them were given enough information—how to use public transportation, how to use money—and eventually they did OK."

When Roger announced to his parents a year later that he and Virginia were "engaged," they responded, almost as a stalling tactic, that to get married he would have to have a job to support himself and his wife.

"Roger can be a dreamer. He gets these ideas in his head, but he doesn't realize the consequences," our father said. "We tried to show him that there was more to marriage than just wanting to do it."

One day, while Roger and some other people from the facility were out on their weekly bowling trip, he slipped away from the group, walked two blocks through the shopping center and into the local branch of a chain of barbeque restaurants. There he applied for a job as a busboy.

"I didn't know how to fill out some things on the card," he remembered. "I had to ask one of the waitresses for help. But she helped me, and then I went back to the others."

Seven months later, the restaurant manager called Roger's residential facility (which was well-known in the community, so there was no secret about his retardation), and hired him.

His current manager, Warren Mays, puts it this way: "The entire restaurant revolves around the work of the busboys. If they're slow, we don't move the customers in and out, the waitresses don't get enough in tips, and we lose money. The industry has a high turnover—nearly 250 percent, meaning that for each slot, two or three people must be hired each year to fill it. The busboy slots turn over very quickly, so we're always looking for people who are going to last," Mays said.

Roger has held the job, at this writing, for more than five years.

Human development sometimes seems like a chariot pulled by a brace of emotional horses, each one charging off in its own direction, at its own speed, though held in place by the reins of intelligence. In my brother's life, his permanent part-time job as a busboy has been his lead stallion, pulling him forward ahead of the other aspects of his life, such as emotional maturity and self-confidence, though they too are in the picture.

"Roger is unique because he doesn't have any prejudice," says Toni Frazier, the waitress he has worked with in the darkened bar area of the restaurant for most of his time there. "If [customers] hurt his feelings [because he's retarded] he reasons his way out, he doesn't take it to heart. If he ever leaves here, I'll probably leave, too. He's just like my brother. I love him."

His job in the bar is to clean the tables off after customers leave, put the placemats, silverware, and napkins in place, and fill the waterglasses and coffee cups of new customers. The bar is a physically small area, about 20 feet long and 10 feet wide, with booths set along the walls. The size of the area has possibly been a factor in Roger's successful managing of his job: It is large enough to require his services, but small enough and with a slow enough customer turnover that he can comprehend everything that is going on.

"He does need a certain amount of understanding that we don't extend to other employees," said his boss, Warren Mays.

"I'll go along with him one step more than with the other people because it takes him longer to understand. You can tell he doesn't readily comprehend, but if you talk slow, using short words, he gets it and he retains it. He doesn't forget."

Whenever things get too hectic for him to handle, however, Roger will disappear off the floor for as long as an hour at a time. He does what he had done at The Queens School in New York when he was six or seven years old—he goes to the bathroom to calm himself down, and waits for the level of action outside to slow down to comprehensible levels.

Toni Frazier finally figured out what he was doing and devised a solution. "I just charge into the bathroom and say, 'Roger, you come right out here. We're busy as sin, and I can't get along without you.' Pretty soon he comes out," she said.

There have been other problems: As his confidence in the job grew, he began to slack off, not wipe the tables as cleanly, and not set the tableware as straight. Warren Mays had a talk with him and got it worked out.

Another time, a steady customer brought his child into the bar and Roger, always fascinated with children, began playing with the baby on the floor. This happened several times; finally Mays took him aside again. "It's always a matter of telling him what the problem is, then letting him tell you his reasons; then, after that, he will listen and respond," Mays said.

There have also been pleasures associated with having the respect of your colleagues. When his residential facility cut back on its staff several years ago, it lost the person who late at night would drive down to the restaurant to pick up Roger after work and take him home. So several of the waitresses got together and worked out an informal carpool, so that someone would drive Roger home each time he worked. "He's that valuable to us," said Toni Frazier. "He helps this place run."

When one of the waiters threw a bachelor party for another waiter, Roger was invited along with everyone else, and got plastered, too.

"The statistics on the number of mentally retarded persons who are employed are hard to come by," said Bernard Posner, director of the President's Committee on Employment of the Handicapped. "People in the work force are not labeled as 'mentally retarded,' they're labeled as workers. So we really don't know. But if we assume that half of the 6.3 million retarded people in the country are adults, and that the employment rate among the retarded is about the same as it is for other handicapped groups—about 40 percent—then we can say, roughly, that 1.2 million retarded adults are working."

Posner's calculations reveal something else. Since approximately nine out of every ten retarded persons are mildly retarded and there are an estimated 2.7 million mildly retarded adults in this country, then 1.5 mildly retarded adults are not working—and they probably could be. Working adults, whether retarded or not, earn money, spend money, pay taxes, and take up less social welfare assistance.

Retarded adults currently hold jobs in restaurants, road crews, mail rooms, industrial situations, hotels and motels, gas stations, hospitals, and schools. The federal government uses what it calls "Schedule A," which has permitted the hiring of about ten thousand retarded and other handicapped persons without the necessity of a civil-service examination.

Some of the Young Turks in the human services field claim that the retarded are encouraged to work in menial or "dirty" jobs only because that is all they are perceived as capable of handling. On the other hand, a group of mildly retarded men is currently employed in the construction industry in California.

Ronald W. Conley, an HEW economist, has shown in his brilliant book, *The Economics of Mental Retardation,* that every dollar invested in the successful vocational training of a retarded male may bring in more than fourteen dollars in lifetime earnings—and the return will never be less than the dollar invested. The results are similar for retarded women.

Mental retardation accounted for a loss of $2.1 billion in 1970 through loss of employment and earnings, according to Conley. That figure might rise to $7 billion if homemaking and other unpaid work is added to this, he wrote.

With every case of moderate, severe, and profound mental retardation that is prevented, $900,000 is saved.

Lifetime custodial care in institutions cost $400,000 (in 1970 dollars).

Roger has always earned the minimum wage, and with his average workweek of twenty hours, he usually grosses about $200 each month (in addition, he gets about $240 each month in Supplemental Security Income).

His method of spending money has been a problem. For years after he started working in the restaurant, he would cash his paycheck, put some of it in a savings account our father had opened for him, and keep the rest of it in his wallet. Once he had more than $100 in it, money that could easily have been lost or stolen.

He used his own funds to buy the books he read and studied, trying to "learn what I didn't learn in school." He bought dictionaries with words he didn't understand; books about the human brain, in which he hoped to find an answer as to why he is retarded; books of history; books on rock collecting and rock 'n' roll, dolls, and toys.

He might be frugal on one end of a shopping trip, asking the bus driver how much the fare was to a certain location, then blow $21 or more on a cab ride home. Roger and Virginia currently have several hundred dollars saved toward the purchase of a home.

Apparently, because he felt he proved himself enough by holding down a part-time job, Roger had not pressed for longer hours.

"Then one day the cat comes to me and says he's getting married," Mays shrugged. "We all know Virginia. Roger would bring her in here and treat her like a queen. He'd introduce her to everybody as his fiancée and it was nice, you know? But then he says he wants more hours, that he wants to work in the dining room, and I had to think about it. I talked to 'Mother,' that's Vee McDowell, the head waitress, but everybody calls her 'Mother,' and she said the girls in the main room were afraid he'd be too slow, that he'd go off the floor too much, that people would have to start doing his work."

Mays sipped coffee as we talked. "I remembered what it was like when I wanted to do something, and everybody else was against it. It was in San Antonio, Texas, in 1960, and I was involved in civil rights then. I was trying to deliberately integrate a bus terminal, and this guy poked a shotgun at me and fired through the glass. He missed, but I kept thinking, 'Hey, look, don't do me any favors. I just want a chance.' I remembered that I got stuck somewhere in my car and I, literally, had to beg for a gallon of gas. So I saw the opposition to him as a matter of prejudice, not of color but of kind. Roger's getting married, he needs the extra money, he's done a good job in the bar; maybe he can hack it in the dining room. I always wanted to do something like this, but I'd never been the boss before. I wanted to give him a chance, but I didn't want to kiss his ass," Mays said.

When a busboy slot on the main floor opened up, Mays told "Mother" he was assigning it to Roger. "I told her, 'trust me' . . . and she did."

"We worried about Roger at first, we really did," Vee McDowell said. "He has to be reminded to do things if it gets slow. But now we depend on him. The problem with busboys is that they can be unreliable, they call you at the last minute and say they're going to a concert or there's a party, or the sun's out, or something like that. We pay the minimum wage, and so we get a lot of school kids. Their sense of responsibility is usually to themselves before us. But Roger is not like that at all. He's nice to the customers, asks them if there's anything they need. He never meets a stranger," she said.

"Look at the way he sets the tables," Mays pointed out. "The napkins are *straight*, and he wipes the crumbs into his busboy's tray, like he's supposed to, and not onto the seats. When a new customer comes in, Roger goes up to them and says, 'Hi, I'm Roger, and I'm your busboy,' something he gets from the waitresses. That helps our image. He hustles from table to table, and sometimes that tray weighs twenty-four to twenty-five pounds. When he takes it into the kitchen, he walks on his tip-toes, because he knows the floors are slippery."

If a heart can ever be said to be bursting with pride, mine nearly burst shortly after talking to Mays when I watched Roger work the main room. Wearing his red busboy's vest, black pants, white shirt, and with a name tag pinned on which read "Roger," he filled the water glasses, filled the coffee cups, wiped the tables clean, lugged his tray into the kitchen, and in Mays' phrase, "kept on truckin'."

My brother may be a man of limited intelligence, but he's not dumb. "He's sharp," said Mays. "He's slickered me. He plays on our attitudes toward him, on the sympathy we give him. Once, after I bawled him out for getting sloppy in his work and getting too friendly with the customers, I started getting telephone calls from people telling me what a great busboy that guy was. 'What's his name?' they'd ask. 'Oh, yeah, Roger,' they'd say, answering their own questions. Then Roger comes up to me one day and says, 'Uh, uh, Warren. [Mays put his fingers together in front of him as Roger does—a very good imitation of my brother.] Have you been hearing anything about my work from the customers?' When I said yes, his face broke out into this big grin and I thought, Why, you little fox, you asked them to call me!"

On another occasion, Bill Stein, one of his former counselors, said Roger invited him to a "birthday party" being given for Roger in the bar one evening. "When I got there I saw all these customers. Each one of them had a present for him! I asked how they found out it was his birthday, and he said he told them. Then when they'd asked, what do you want, he'd told them that too, apparently telling each person something different so there wouldn't be any duplicate presents. You should have seen what he got—games, a shirt, record albums. He's something."

During my several visits to the restaurant to interview people, I often sat with Roger at a table in the back of the bar. He would introduce me to people he worked with—the waitresses and busboys and some of the steady customers—but he was always pretty cool about it, holding back the emotions I know he feels. But when he saw Warren Mays come into the room, he got visibly excited, then sort of casually waved "Hi" to him. He had to literally choke back his enthusiasm. I realized that a brother is always a brother, but having a boss is an achievement.

The restaurant became a major part of his world; its clanking glasses and overloaded trays give him life lines to the world of the nonretarded, the world of the nondevalued, the world of the appreciated. He has a healthy self-image, which was nurtured by our parents, and reinforced by his presence at the restaurant and by Virginia, who proudly sat next to him at the facility and who often did his laundry, since as a "working man" he was too busy to do it himself. (The counselors worked on stopping her, since Roger was taking advantage of Virginia's desire for an independent identity, and was at the same time not developing a full concept of self-reliance.)

One of the privileges of restaurant work, traditionally, has been a discount on the price of food purchased, and Roger liked to work his schedule so he took as many meals as possible there (this also got him out of the facility for a longer period of time).

Having a hamburger or barbeque ribs with Toni Frazier or "Mother" McDowell or Harmonica John (one of the cooks) or even by himself, Roger was a regular fellow. He was a guy who worked there, an employee, a social security number, a name on a time sheet, a busboy, somebody with a red vest. He was not retarded, not as his principal definition. He was not handicapped, not as far as his ability to pay taxes was concerned. He was not helpless and hopeless, not as far as the colleagues who relied on him were concerned. He was simply another employee who got a couple of bucks knocked off the price of a meal.

Marc Gold, a behavior-modification researcher who has sold programs he has developed for training the severely and profoundly retarded to several states and government agencies, has coined what he calls the competency/deviancy hypothesis. Simply stated, it means that the more competence an individual has, the more deviancy will be tolerated by others.

Gold's hypothesis is intriguing, because it speaks directly to two images of Roger at this time: one, sitting in the restaurant in which he works, a competent employee having a meal; the other, in his room back at the facility, unable to talk to his fiancée without the door to his room or her room being left open, playing the phonograph records from his childhood over and over again, watching cartoons on television, and shaking his hands when he gets excited.

The two images align themselves to show that mental retardation is not a fixed, unchanging condition, but a dynamic one that can change through time. Mental retardation does not refer to all of an individual's functional abilities, but only to some. Retarded people can, and do, take their place in society.

"Once Virginia had an operation on her ankle," recalled "Mother" McDowell, "and Roger wheeled her over here in a wheelchair" from the apartments half a mile away in which they then lived. "He clucked over her all afternoon, and when she wanted to go the ladies' room, he wheeled her to the door and then some of the waitresses helped her inside."

One night, several years before he had moved into the community and while he was still living at the facility, one of the waitresses asked him for a date. As he tells it: "She had been married six times before, and wanted to go out dancing." Presumably she was looking for hubby number seven. "So we went out, and stayed out a long time. I had a stinger and we went dancing, and I got dizzy. Then we went back to her apartment, and stayed just a few minutes, because she had a child, and then she tried to drive me back to the home, but we got lost and I didn't get back until two in the morning," he said proudly.

Although nothing untoward happened at the woman's house, it was not long after this that Virginia paid her visit to the restaurant. In addition to hearing this tale of her fiancée's high-flying nightlife, she learned that there were not only busboys at the restaurant, but busgirls, too.

"I was jealous until I talked to each of them and found out that they all had boyfriends," she said.

Virginia saw to it that there was no more late-night monkey business with husband-hunting waitresses.

When the Washington *Post* series on Roger and Virginia was being published, I had to call my brother to check up on some facts. He took the occasion to ask me which pictures of him would be published. I pulled the old dodge that reporters don't have any control of the art with their pictures, but he didn't buy it. "Why don't you publish the picture of me in the restaurant? It's important, Bobby."

He kept saying it was important, though he didn't say why, but by the urgent tone in his voice, I knew he was on to something. As I thought about it, I realized he was right: It was important that he had a job that he had gotten himself, that he had kept it through several changes of managers and various shifts of waitresses, and that he had gotten himself extra work time in the main dining room by proving to his boss that he was worthy of it.

The picture to which he referred—one showing him carrying an armload of dishes through the crowded restaurant, wearing his red vest and plastic bow tie—spoke volumes about the ability of retarded people to work, successfully, in the community. I knew the picture had not been scheduled for publication, but Roger had made a telling point. When I hung up, I saw *Post* Managing Editor Howard Simons walking across the newsroom. Simons had been an early supporter of the series. I explained Roger's feelings about the picture, and said I agreed with my brother. Simons went over to the photo desk, and the picture ran on page one the next morning.

 **14**

RAIN

Rain, rain coming down
From sad clouds. The ground
becomes wet, and yet it grows trees,
Weeds, and flowers from seeds, and so
the clouds are happy anyway to grow them.

The rain is wet like morning dew,
and yet you can smell its fresh air.

The rain goes pitter padder on my
window sill. The rain water is forming
a puddle. Rain drops hit the puddle.
A ripple forms, big and bigger, until it ends.
But more rain drops are falling, more ripples
   are forming, one after another
Looking like round rings.

As we both see our own reflection
in a puddle of rain water,
we were made to love each other.
For love cannot hide anytime.
But when we move away with our
reflection there's no more reflection.

Then the rain goes away. The puddle dries up.
The sun comes up. And there is always love.

—ROGER MEYERS

During this period of the 1970s, I was again having difficulties with my parents. I was beginning a career as a freelance writer and was newly married. There was enough in my life to occupy me, without the continuing and seemingly never-ending problems of my parents and brother.

As a stringer for the *Post* in Los Angeles, I had handled some assignments in connection with the Watergate investigation—political sabotage and "dirty tricks" done against Democrats in Los Angeles, San Diego, and elsewhere, particularly those involving Donald H. Segretti (Segretti later pleaded guilty to mail fraud in connection with activities in Florida). My coup was finding an attorney friend of Segretti's who gave us a sworn statement that Segretti had told him he had been hired for the dirty tricks campaign by Dwight Chapin, then President Nixon's appointments secretary. (Chapin was later convicted of lying to a Federal grand jury about his knowledge of Segretti's activities.)

I was very proud of my work, and of its description in Woodward and Bernstein's book, *All the President's Men*, which was published in the spring of 1974. But try as I might, I couldn't get my parents to read it—not at publication, and not until six months had passed.

"What is it I have to do to get you to pay attention to me?" I yelled at them one night, pounding on the table. "This involves the President of the United States—would you read about me if I had investigated God?"

There were explanations, plausible, businesslike, but none of them worked: They had known all along what I was doing; they were very proud of me anyway. But the only explanation that I believed then or now is that they couldn't handle the idea of my independence and maturity.

The Special Olympics gave my parents an additional chance to help what they were now referring to as "the cause." Whenever the events were held in Los Angeles County, my father could volunteer to write press releases, and my mother volunteer to line up Hollywood "personalities" whose presence would guarantee the appearance of the television news cameras whose coverage was so important to convincing the public that the retarded are really not so different from other people.

Once our mother had talked to total strangers about her

plans to start a residential facility for the retarded. Now she began talking to the cameramen, the news producers, the secretaries, and the hangers-on she met in the Los Angeles TV business about what a great idea it would be to produce a documentary about mental retardation. She wanted to show people that it really wasn't a crime to have a retarded person in the family, and if they liked she could send them some material she had accumulated on the subject, or would they like to meet her son, Roger, who wrote poetry?

"The gambit worked," she said. "A producer became interested, and she made a documentary about the retarded, focusing in on Roger, and the facility where he and Virginia lived."

The program borrowed its title from one of Roger's poems, called "Standing Strong," which Roger recited on camera. (Roger still didn't get a publisher for his poems, something she could not understand.)

That TV show, which was later nominated for a local Emmy award, was filmed in part at the regional finals of the 1973 Special Olympics in Los Angeles. Showing the cheerfully brazen attitude which she had developed, our mother not only had Roger in the documentary, but got him placed in a lead car as it circled the UCLA cinder track at Drake Stadium. Inside the car, as the Grand Marshal for the events, was TV star David Cassidy—who'd been a student at the junior high school where other students had tormented and harassed Roger.

There were photos aplenty, and because David Cassidy was in the picture, Roger's picture was published in several teeny-bopper fan magazines, along with the poem he wrote Cassidy on his birthday.

Along with David Cassidy came his mother, actress Shirley Jones.

Somehow, Shirley Jones ended up presenting an "award" to Roger for his work "on behalf of the retarded." The award was presented at a fancy black-tie ball at the Beverly Hills Hotel. At the same annual ball put on by the group of older, wealthy CAMEO people who raised money for the facility where Roger and Virginia lived, astronaut Edwin Mitchell, "the sixth man on the moon," congratulated Roger, who stood there right along with him. When Mitchell introduced Roger, he also introduced Virginia, as Roger's "girlfriend."

"Oh, no," Virginia interrupted. "I'm his fiancée. Want to see the ring?" With that she held up her hand, on which was the pearl that symbolized their union.

Our parents wanted Roger recognized for his achievements; so he "won" awards that had never been presented before. But his real achievements, his job and his developing personal life, were left largely untouched as subject matter for honors.

Our parents liked the media attention, I believe, because it helped compensate for the stigma from which they had suffered for so long and because by eliminating the stigma attached to mental retardation they could help other parents in years to come.

On July 1, 1970—several months after Roger had moved into his residential facility—an innovative approach to the concept of delivering services to the retarded was launched in Nebraska. Called ENCOR (Eastern Nebraska Community Office of Retardation), it was designed to fill the gaps between existing services for retarded citizens, offer them a wide variety of alternative methods of living and work, and provide models for the retarded and their families. It is one of the "proofs of the pudding" of the legislation in this field.

According to Frank J. Menolascino, M.D., one of the designers of the ENCOR program and the president of NARC between 1976 and 1978, the idea was "to provide a comprehensive continuum of services at the local level, so that no retarded person should ever have to leave the ENCOR region to receive the services he might need."

With the ENCOR program (and others like it), these are some of the residential options available: children's residences, family-like homes, adult residences, family living residences, adult-training residences, adult board and room homes under minimum supervision, and independent living arrangements with supervision and guidance available as needed.

The ENCOR program also includes work-training programs in industry (*not* in sheltered workshops), and summer job-training programs. ENCOR stresses volunteer community action, including a program in which parents of retarded persons give advice and information to other parents who have just realized that their child is retarded.

Such structured, organized approaches to dealing with mentally retarded citizens do not automatically solve all problems. A change in attitude in which retarded citizens are seen as people, not as crippled objects, is necessary as well. For example, the vice president of a well-known residential facility told me his interest in retarded people had developed out of his "Christian concern" for them. As we entered the workshop building, on a tour of the facilities, a black-haired woman resident in her thirties started talking to my guide, complaining about another resident, who she claimed was picking on her. I thought that she was showing what I previously learned are signs of so-called institutional behavior—in her case, talking to strangers about subjects they know nothing about.

As the woman talked on, the man of "Christian concern" began backing away from her as if she was a leper. His face had a frozen look, his mouth was downturned with disgust. It would have been comical if it hadn't been so sad.

I saw another example of poor attitude, at a workshop which employs the profoundly and severely retarded (I.Q. levels between 18 and 40) in state-of-the-art electronic circuitry, where they do subcontracting work for the National Aeronautics and Space Administration (NASA). The attitude of one of the counselors troubled me. After guiding me around the facility, she said, in front of some retarded people, that she would now introduce me to "the staff." Her voice clearly indicated that nonstaff people were dismissed. All but one of the workers left, and my guide introduced me to everyone, except the retarded man in his forties *who was standing next to her.* Since I was there to learn how the staff was helping the retarded, and not how the staff was helping itself, I leaned past the woman, put my hand out, and said, "What's this man's name?"

" 'ARRY!" was the reply, and when we shook hands Larry's smile lit up the room. Then *having been recognized,* Larry got his coat and left.

I have spent most of my life thinking of my brother as my "retarded" brother, not understanding his stubbornness, integrity, and ability to handle an independent (or almost independent) life, and not realizing how much we have in common. The thinking and research I undertook for the newspaper series began to open my mind.

One evening in Baltimore, someone who did not know my family asked what my brother did. I started to reply that he is retarded. Suddenly it struck me for the first time in the twenty-eight years of our lives together that mental slowness is not the sum of his existence. He is a man who is married, holds down a job, pays taxes, and writes poetry. I hope I will never forget that moment: I was in my car, driving down a dark street in Baltimore, and I'd been asked what my brother does.

I replied that he is in the restaurant business.

 **15**

WINDOW

I'm looking at my window from outdoors,
looking at the reflection of snow, white like fur
through the cold watery air.
The likeness of snow is made from up there,
From so many waterdrops into white
crystal rocks. Falling down they hop one by one
on my window and window sill. The snow man took
   his pill.

I can see the likeness of snow, looking at my window
its beauty rich, that surrounds love.
You can look at any window, the image of Santa Claus
who came from the South Pole

I can see snow melting like an image of love,
Melting with warm water rolling down the window.

The window I'm looking at I see the reflection
   of morning dew,
On the grass, flowers popping up fast.
I'm looking at my window cause as you can see
window is made from glass.

—ROGER MEYERS

First the ground was cleared, then the wooden supports were laid down, then the concrete was poured. Roger and Virginia watched the apartments going up on the acres their facility owned with excitement and fear: As soon as the structures were completed, they would be among the first persons to move from the large complex buildings—twenty-five persons under one roof; don't shut the door if you've got somebody with you—to apartments of their own. They would move there under the auspices of their facility's Transitional Living Project. The project was possible because of newly-available federal money. One counselor would always live within the garden-style apartment buildings; he would be ready to help with such things as grocery shopping, the need to wash dishes after every meal, and what to do when the drain gets clogged.

"We taught by demonstration and by role-playing, by going into such things as cooking, money, the use of public transportation, grocery lists, bargains, and legal rights, since the retarded have the same rights as anyone else," said Hank Newman, a counselor from the facility who was intimately involved with the Transitional Living Project.

"At the beginning, Virginia was more advanced than Roger, though a year before she couldn't discuss her physical disability, her speech problems, or things like that. She had taken charge of her life more than Roger had, perhaps because Roger had always had more things done for him by his family. Virginia has fewer outside interests than Roger, and more of an interest in getting herself together. Initially, I wasn't too sure how motivated Roger was to be fully independent," Newman said.

In their apartments, there were intensified lessons in cooking, in housecleaning, laundry, and budgeting. There were mistakes—overcooked meals, dust where you would most expect it, too much bleach in the wash, too little money saved, too much spent on novelty items.

Virginia, who her counselors felt had never been living up to her true potential, began making wonderful progress. She made conscious efforts at not babying Roger, something that often ignited his volatile temper. She learned to handle criticism of herself better than she had before, learned to talk about her disabilities, and to work around them. She energetically pursued a work rehabilitation program, which, though it did not lead, immediately, to employment, gave her additional real-world experience of the kind she needed.

Roger made some progress along with his spaghetti suppers (to which he often treated Virginia). But he also developed a very common response to the stresses he was facing: He began overeating by gargantuan amounts, adding sugar and cream to already sweetened coffee, finding whatever was fattening and gooey in stores and restaurants and wolfing it down. During the months he lived in the semi-independent apartments, he gained twenty-five pounds. Shortly after moving to an apartment of his own, he gained another twenty-five pounds. In order to fit into his wedding suit, he dieted and exercised and lost thirty pounds. Some of this came back during the early months of marriage, but as Roger and Virginia settled down, it quickly melted away.

Roger was not the only one feeling stress, however; our parents were having the damnedest time adjusting to the idea that Roger was living "virtually" by himself, even though a counselor also lived in the same building.

"We were concerned about his health, concerned that maybe things were moving too quickly," our father said. "We didn't want him to get hurt."

The other side of this coin was that Roger would start slowing himself down after visiting with his parents.

"Whenever I'd talk to him during the week, he'd be anxious to try the next step, get his own apartment, become really independent," Bill Stein recalled. "Then he'd see your parents on the weekends, and on Mondays he wouldn't be too sure. He'd hesitate; he'd fall back into those old habits."

Roger's weight and budgeting problems were blamed by our father on Roger's counselors, who he said were not doing their job, and were not giving him all the help he needed. He included Stein in this criticism, even as he was coming to rely on him more and more.

Roger and Virginia never made these criticisms. James Clements, M.D., the former head of the American Association on Mental Deficiency, says that criticism is a common response when the traditional parenting roles are handled by surrogates, such as counselors.

"Parents have a hard time accepting that someone else can do their job, that someone else might know more about a particular situation than themselves," he said.

Where once our mother worried that she would never find a place where Roger would be taken care of, now she worried that in his semi-independent apartment life, Roger wouldn't be able to take care of himself.

"I would go down there and help him with his housekeeping chores, like I always did. I'd move his papers around, clean the stove and try without success to get him to save his money—not spend it on toys or school books or records," she said.

Mother would see his incredible intensity to learn "what I missed in school," and be unable to persuade him not to spend what, in effect, were his lower-class earnings on his middle-class ambitions.

"I bought *The Promise of American Democracy*," he told her one day, holding up a copy of a popular work. "I paid seventy-four cents for it at the K-Mart."

After these visits Mother would be so tense, she could not eat for hours. Often, after Roger's weekend visits to their apartment, she would spend the following day in bed, resting. She attributed these problems to "stress and strain."

It soon became clear to Bill Stein and the other counselors that Roger and Virginia, and about half a dozen other retarded persons living in the semi-independent units, could almost surely succeed in the least structured environment possible— their own apartments in the community.

Hank Newman, like Stein and Carol Knieff, a counselor of the same age as Roger and Virginia themselves, was delegated the task of finding apartments for this group of people of whom so little had ever been expected and by whom so much had been achieved.

"I wanted the apartments to be in the community where we already lived, because that community was familiar with the residents from our home, and the residents themselves were used to the community," Newman said.

As had been the case with funds for the semi-independent living units, the monthly rental fees could be paid out of the

Supplemental Security Income (SSI) funds Roger, Virginia, and the others received each month.

Newman compiled a list of apartment complexes in the area. Much to his surprise, he found acceptance at the first complex he visited.

"We don't rent to them to be good; we do it because it's good business," said Charles Tracy, who manages the 215-unit building with his wife, Anita. After discussions with Newman about the functional ability (quite good) of the people Newman wanted to see move in, the Tracys agreed to take all seven people he recommended. Three of them (including Roger) moved into apartments by themselves; four others (including Virginia) shared apartments, two in each one. Roger's rent for a furnished two-bedroom apartment was just under $200 a month.

"They are our best tenants," said Anita Tracy. "They always pay their rent at least one day ahead of time, and they don't give us any trouble at all. Sometimes they get upset when the little things go wrong: when the drain backs up or the lights don't work. They complain just like anyone else when someone is playing music too loud, something like that. This is their big chance, and they don't want to lose it. What's humdrum for us is special for them," she said.

Roger's apartment is on the first floor (after their honeymoon, Virginia moved into it from her apartment on the far side of the complex). It is filled with reminders of the known and familiar. Along one wall, he put his desk and a bookcase for his schoolbooks, "where I study to make up what I missed in school," he says. There is a small table for meals, and a kitchen with an electric stove, double sink, and refrigerator. When he was a bachelor, Roger used one of the two bedrooms as his "schoolroom," where he had a portable blackboard with such exercises as $56 + 3 = 59$ written on it in white chalk. The room also housed his Hoola-hoops, TV magazines, discarded toys and dolls, a bicycle he bought at Sears but rarely rides, clothes, and boxes. In the bedroom closet, he kept his work clothes—black pants, white shirts, and red vests—all neatly lined up, and away from his other clothes.

On one wall, he has fan magazine pictures of TV stars he likes (David Cassidy among them), and also photographs of young children he has met in his life. They are always autographed: "To Roger, my best friend."

Robert B. Edgerton, in his book *The Cloak of Competence,* traces the histories of 110 adults who once had been interned at Pacific State Hospital. The mean I.Q. level was about 65, the length of hospital stay about twenty years. In a chapter entitled, "Passing and Denial," he described how many people interviewed had purchased and displayed pictures of people they did not know, and had photograph albums of people to whom they were not related. Others collected china cups and saucers as a sign of their "family connections." For these people, such items were attempts to cover up the long years of hospital confinement and the fact that they did not have any true family connections.

For Roger, his photographs are not only mementos of friends he has made, but proof that he is accepted by people whose company he enjoyed. The fact that these people are children may be because children are the people with whom he feels most comfortable, who demand the least of him, and to whom he can respond the most fully.

There are, of course, pictures of Roger's and Virginia's own families in the apartment, to which each of them point with pride.

Manager Charles Tracy was initially concerned about what impact the presence of retarded people would have on his other tenants. He concluded it was no different from the impact of any other minority group moving into the complex.

"At the beginning, I watched them [Roger and Virginia] and the other [retarded] tenants like a hawk. But it was like when we first rented to black people: No one pays any attention to them."

His wife added: "Now they mingle with the other tenants just like anyone else, talk about soap powder, things like that. Roger hustles out to the laundry room, takes out the trash, or takes a swim in the pool. It's just like anyone else."

Because every small action taken by the retarded often requires a major exercise in logistics, there have been lumps in the smooth operation of their apartment-living adventure. "Roger used to forget his door key so often we finally suggested he get a retractable key ring which he could wear on his belt, so he wouldn't lose his key," Anita Tracy said. That key ring travels with him everywhere.

Once before his marriage, Mrs. Tracy saw Roger struggling home on a humid day carrying a bag of groceries—which somehow slipped out of his arms and crashed to the cement.

"He came in here all excited, all flustered, not knowing what to do. He said he was late for work, but that the groceries were all over the street, and he was just all upset. The first thing I told him to do was calm down, and take off his jacket. I don't know why he was wearing it on a day like that anyway. [Our mother's training, which I must still periodically struggle against, too.] Then I told him he probably wasn't the first person in the world to be late to work, and that he should call ahead, tell them what had happened, and say he would be in as soon as possible. He looked at me, incredulous. 'You mean I can do that?' The thought had never entered his mind. After that I gave him some shopping bags, and he went out and scooped up his groceries."

On another occasion, when it was pouring rain, the Tracys' daughter offered to drive Roger back to the residential facility where he had formerly lived, and where he still worked as a teacher's aide. He accepted.

Mrs. Tracy recalled, "Shortly afterward, Roger started coming in here and saying he had missed his bus to the place, and could our daughter please give him a ride? But I knew the bus schedule, and knew he hadn't missed his bus—he was just trying to get a free ride." As he had done with Warren Mays at the restaurant, Roger tried to play on people's sympathy for him to make life easier for himself. In this case he ended up back at the bus stop.

Bill Stein was, initially, worried about the choice of the apartment complex, which was located across the street from a schoolyard. "I thought, My God, you know the old prejudice about the retarded, one of those people is going to wander over there and somebody is going to yell, *'Pervert!'* " Stein's concern has proved groundless, but this is an interesting example of the sensitivity that workers with the retarded now bring to their field.

The two-bedroom apartment Virginia shared with another woman was kept immaculately clean, dishes were washed as soon as they were used, beds were made every morning, crumbs were wiped off the dining table, and pictures of her family were positioned neatly on the end tables. Her willingness to handle the homemaking details for both herself and her husband worried her counselors before the marriage.

"Roger has a tendency to let others do things for him," Carol Knieff said. "But it's best for his development if he does things for himself."

For example, Roger's kitchen floor was always dirty, and, after failing several times at cleaning it, he gave up. "I would wash it, but then I couldn't get the hard dirt and smear off," he said. During a meeting with Carol Knieff and Virginia he said that he really didn't have to do that, now, "because Virginia can do that after we're married."

Carol investigated and discovered that "he was using a cleanser which left its own film on the floor."

"Then I used Mr. Clean and it was better," Roger said.

Because of this, I was surprised when I visited their apartment four months after the wedding, and saw my male chauvinist brother *cleaning up the kitchen.* "I didn't think he did much housework," I remarked offhandedly to Virginia.

If looks could kill, I would have been a goner. "He does a lot more than anyone knows," she said. "He just needs time to do things his own way."

Keeping herself and her apartment neat and clean are part of what Virginia calls the "good grooming habits, needed for everyone."

They buy groceries at the local supermarket, where her gregarious husband quickly learns everyone's name. For emergencies there is the 7-Eleven, two blocks away. Whenever they need to, they go to a local bank and spend five dollars for a book of tickets to a subsidized taxi service. For this wonderful service, they call a number, and the driver comes to their door. Sometimes he comes right away, and sometimes it takes as long as an hour. But the service gives them access to their community (they can take the bus now, but bus routes are limited). Because of this service, in which each gives the driver a ticket worth fifty cents for a ride, they can go to weekend movies, or to a restaurant, or to visit friends, or go shopping when it rains.

Carol Knieff says that these activities mean "they are making good use of their community, learning to live within it." I was struck by how much of it is helped by this unique form of personal transportation, which in other cities is usually geared only toward the elderly.

Especially now that they are moving within the community, neither one likes being called "retarded." "I don't like being labeled 'retarded,' I don't like it," Virginia told me. "We're not that dumb, we're slow-minded, but we're not that dumb. You can see how far we've come. To a certain extent I am slow, but that's why I like the simple life. We just say we're slow-minded people, which is a better way of saying it. Anything to cover up the word 'retarded,'" she said.

My marriage ended in August 1975, as Roger and Virginia continued to plan their own. Although the strains on our parents continued, their pressures were no longer as monolithic as they once seemed. Roger was getting out on his own, attitudes had changed, he was getting older, and he would outlive them in a world less bleak than it had once appeared.

I have my brother's struggle for independence to thank for the fact that our parents no longer see him as the weak fourth member of the family, who must be supported by the other three. Not entirely, maybe not even willingly, and certainly not without a fight, but the fact was that my parents had also begun to see me as an independent person—a son and not a second father, a strong young man rather than a strong right arm, a person of my own.

So when my marriage ended, they were warmer and more

sympathetic to me than at any other time in our lives. Because of the humiliating experiences during my early college years and because of their hesitation at fully acknowledging me or my accomplishments, I had tended to keep my personal life away from them. They knew this, but acknowledged it to themselves only secretly. Shortly after telling my parents that my marriage had ended, and while sitting in their living room, I found myself, at the age of thirty-two, crying on my mother's shoulder. It was a unique experience, a painful and ultimately a healthy one, but one which would not have been possible just a few years previously.

The business of living alone can create problems, Roger discovered: There are all those steps, each carrying with it its own hazards; decisions must be made at every point, and if they are not then problems arise. Returning from the market, he put everything neatly away, as he had seen his own mother do, as he had seen his counselors do, as Virginia did in her apartment. Roger put everything in the cupboards and in the refrigerator, though not necessarily those items that belonged there. He put a package of hamburger meat in the cupboard, and when our mother found it there the following week, the horror of what it smelled like lingered in her mind.

On another occasion he decided to make pancakes one Saturday morning. He bought the pancake mix, milk, and the eggs needed for the recipe, as well as the pancake syrup, which he liked to pour over the finished product as if it were going out of style. He made up the batter, got the grill to just the right temperature, so that tiny clouds of steam arose from it, and poured the batter into perfectly small round circles. Then he turned the flame low, so the pancakes would not burn. Then Roger decided to watch a morning TV show and left the pancakes cooking on the stove.

A neighbor saw smoke pouring out Roger's living-room window, and called the fire department. They arrived minutes later and pounded on Roger's door, which he quickly opened. He'd heard their sirens and seen the flashing lights and been fascinated as the engine truck had pulled up in front of his apartment building; then he watched as the helmeted firemen charged into his apartment.

What was the problem, he wanted to know? After all, there was smoke, but no fire. . . .

These are not two examples of the incompetence of retarded people, or of their inability to lead independent lives. They are examples of the difficulties they face every day, and of what can happen when what others perceive as common ordinary procedures are forgotten or skipped. They are also examples of mistakes Roger no longer makes.

Once Charles and Anita Tracy decided to rent apartments to retarded citizens, they also decided not to treat them any differently from anyone else. Therefore the seven apartments rented to the retarded adults were scattered through the sprawling, 2-story, 215-unit complex. "We do that so there's a good mix. We scatter young people, old people, blacks, Mexicans, all like that. That way people mix more and it makes for better tenants," Charles Tracy said.

Tracy also recalled meeting a Down's Syndrome man who was visiting one of his tenants. The man asked Tracy if he too could rent an apartment.

"I told him he could, as soon as Hank Newman said he was ready, and I mean it. I like to work with the counselors because they know the ones who can handle it and the ones who can't. But you should have seen that guy's face light up. Just the idea that maybe, someday, he might be able to live here, why, it was hope for the hopeless. And how many other retarded people are there who might be able to do this, if they are given half a chance? I often wonder about that," he said.

Shortly before Roger's wedding, Charles Tracy was standing by the rack of mail boxes, talking with a prospective tenant, when the soon-to-be-married Virginia Hensler came up. "She was about to change the name on the mail box from just 'Roger Meyers' to 'Mr. and Mrs. R. Meyers,' and she was so excited she couldn't contain herself. Really. She was laughing and giggling and acting like a little girl, though, of course, you can't blame her. But I was wondering what effect it would have on this woman, seeing that here was a tenant who was retarded."

Would the ghost of Henry Goddard come back to haunt them both? Would the prejudice against the retarded—against their *presence*—lose him a paying tenant?

"It didn't bother her a bit. She rented a nice one-bedroom apartment."

16

LOOKING THROUGH DARK

I am looking through the dark and
What do I see? I see nothing which
Is around me.

This is something, being inside
I can't hear no sound, it is just dark
as dark as dark can be. If I was outside
at night I would see trees that would
look like maybe monsters that would
look real but yet it isn't real at all.

I can feel the magic crystal ball with
stars and the moon around the sky, but it is
more than just a magic crystal ball, it is
God's universe, this is God's light reflecting
through dark, seeing many shadows that
may look mysterious but they are only people
standing still.

I can see my shadow.
Shadows aren't really that mysterious.
Could I be alone, looking through the dark?
Oh no, that could never be, because God is
Omnipotent, Supreme, and I am with
God's light always.

—ROGER MEYERS

In early January 1978, in a wealthy section of Silver Spring, Maryland, someone fired a shotgun blast through the living-room window of a home occupied by two employed retarded adults, and two nonretarded adult counselors. The blast, for which no one has ever been arrested, was a violent form of community protest against the location of a group home in a residential community. The plans for the group home, called Jubilee House, were to house no more than eight mildly retarded adults, plus staff, in a fifteen-room, $120,000 house on a half-acre of land. Despite the fact that three other group homes are in existence in the area, unwarranted community fears led to the shotgun blast, as well as burning rags tossed at the house and telephone calls with heavy breathing on the line at all hours of the day and night.

"There are still many problems in the field, many people who don't understand what mental retardation is, or who the mentally retarded are," said James Clements, M.D., when I spoke with him in Atlanta, three months before the shotgun blast. "You've got to put some of this bad news in your book, or else Roger's and Virginia's story is going to sound like a fairy tale."

It has not been hard filling a manila folder full of bad news articles and interviews. Here are some of the low lights:

• On October 3, 1977, the Comptroller General of the United States issued a report to the Congress stating: "No Federal agency is co-ordinating a national strategy to prevent mental retardation or directing Federal resources toward prevention."

• On January 7, 1977, another report by the Comptroller General stated: ". . . many mentally disabled persons have been released from institutions before sufficient community facilities and services were available and without adequate planning and follow-up. Others enter, remain in, or re-enter institutions unnecessarily."

• There is little co-ordination of the myriad governmental regulations concerning retarded persons. For example, one section of the 1974 Federal Housing Act provides "housing assistance payments" for low-income people, including the mentally handicapped. But the Supplemental Security Income regulations put a ceiling on how much "unearned income" an SSI recipient can receive before he loses his SSI money—thus canceling out the impact of the housing-assistance money.

• Attempts to open alternative-living facilities (such as the one in Maryland) often meet community opposition. The stated opposition somehow always comes down to the fear that retarded individuals are going to be raping daughters or seducing sons, when they are not lowering property values. The fight often involves interpretations of residential zoning laws, and whether they permit several nonrelated individuals to live together as "families." Proponents have several times won on the grounds that denying the retarded people permission to live in a community in a group home is a denial of their due process and equal-protection rights.

• The way the Supplemental Security Income law is written discourages retarded adults from finding employment at which they earn more than $200 each month. For example, Roger recently was offered four additional hours of work at his restaurant. Had he accepted, his gross weekly pay would have gone up by no more than $10, but his monthly total would have risen above the $200 cutoff point. At that point he would have lost, irrevocably, the roughly $240 in monthly SSI funds, as well as—most importantly—the availability to him of counseling. In short, by increasing his earnings by $40, he would have lost more than $240 in aid. Such a law actually amounts to a "disincentive to work," according to Bernard Posner, head of the President's Committee on Employment of the Handicapped. It broke Roger's heart to tell Warren Mays he couldn't take the extra hours.

• Although 1 percent of the general population is regarded as retarded at any one time, at least 10 percent of the prison population in this country is retarded. Yet there usually are no special services or training for the retarded in prison, and retarded people in prison are often victimized by other prisoners.

• Accurate information about mental retardation is still not known by people involved in life-or-death decisions in hospitals concerning retarded infants. In 1968, Joseph Fletcher, Ph.D., currently a Visiting Professor of Bio-Medical Ethics at the University of Virginia School of Medicine, wrote in the *Atlantic Monthly* magazine that a father grieving over his decision to withhold medical help from his Down's Syndrome baby should not feel guilty because ". . . true guilt arises only from an offense against a person, and a Down's is not a person." When I spoke with him in January 1978, Fletcher said he had not known that a year before his article, a book entitled *The Diary of Nigel Hunt* had been published. It was written by a man who is a Down's Syndrome person. Fletcher now says he would amend his position to say that medical aid should be withheld from infants with an I.Q. of "plus or minus 20," who also have significant functional disabilities. Robert E. Cooke, M.D., president of the Medical College of Pennsylvania, however, says that it is impossible to tell during the first few months of life what an infant's I.Q. is going to be, and that many current and future technical advances could be used to remedy significant functional problems. Fletcher said that since his article, "I have learned that a wide spectrum of mental retardation is not susceptible to generalization."

• One family physician, who advises parents, declined to be interviewed for this book, saying, "I don't think publicity should be brought to this field. I don't know how to explain it, and I wish them well, but when I take my kids to the circus I don't go to the side show."

In late 1976, Virginia's mother saw an ad placed by a store that sold wedding dresses. The dresses were on sale. Virginia's mother didn't really know when or if her daughter would be getting married, but she knew a good buy when she saw one. She bought a beautiful gown, and when Virginia came to visit her at Christmas, had her fitted for it.

"I bought the gown for Virginia's trousseau. I wanted her to look beautiful when she got married," she said.

The "when," of course, was thought to be far off in the future. (Bill Stein says it's a common experience to meet retarded people in institutional or custodial settings and find out they're engaged. "You ask them when they got engaged and they say, 'Oh, 1927'.") But at least Virginia would have something to look forward to; she'd have a trousseau just like all the other young daughters of all the better families. When she was ready for marriage, the dress would be ready for her.

Virginia, however, didn't see it that way. "I didn't know what a 'trousseau' was," she said. "I just knew my momma had bought me the dress."

Several days later, back at her apartment, Virginia met with Roger and excitedly discussed this unexpected turn of events. Whenever they'd discussed marriage, they'd always said they would be married on an Easter Sunday, to mark the anniversary of their first baby-sitting assignment with Virginia's nephew, Scottie. He is the child with nongenetic cerebral palsy of whom they had taken such good care.

Easter Sunday was also an important date for them because the resurrection of Jesus Christ, they felt, was an important statement about life and new beginnings, a concept they fervently embraced.

"We looked on the calendar, and saw that the next Easter Sunday was on April 10. So that's when we decided to get married. When I told my momma, she did what every other mother does, she cried," Virginia recalled.

They had *told* their parents; they had not *asked* permission.

"Well, of course we were concerned; we were concerned when you said you were getting married," our father recalled. "What parent wouldn't be? But there was nothing we could do. They had made up their minds, and you know Rogie when he sets his mind on something, he's stubborn as he can be. The counselors all thought they could handle it. It's part of that 'normalization' thing, and why shouldn't they have the right to marry just like anyone else? When they told us, it was a *fait accompli*, so to speak."

Virginia's mother knew this young beau of her daughter's, and knew once Virginia had set her sights on him there was no turning her around. She had seen them together, seen their developing maturity, seen their reliance on each other when there was no one else, and seen that when the frustrations of being mentally retarded became great (and they did, frequently), they each had the ability to reassure and comfort the other.

"One day Virginia and I went out shopping, but we got

delayed coming back. Roger was supposed to be with Virginia that night, and when we returned he was so mad he started throwing things around his apartment. Finally he stormed out.

"Virginia was the only one who could handle him," her mother said. "She went right outside, found him, and calmed him down."

When I visited their apartment, recently, I saw the opposite side of this coin. Virginia was washing the dishes, and a yellow plastic drinking cup slipped down the drain. It was a perfect fit, and was perfectly stuck.

Virginia tried to get it out, using her fingers, her hand, then a fork. When she couldn't get it out, she started complaining, "Oh, it's stuck, I don't know what to do. This always happens when Roger's not around." She walked around the kitchen, complaining, making nervous gestures, and picking at her skin.

I tried to get the cup out of the drain and failed. Roger had been in the living room and came over to see what the problem was. Virginia told him. Roger went over to the sink, stuck his hand in the drain, did something with his fingers, and the cup came out.

He laughed in triumph, and Virginia beamed, then sighed, and settled back to her housekeeping.

It is a mark of how little is popularly known about mental retardation, today, that several otherwise well-informed people asked me after the newspaper series if Roger and Virginia were the first mildly retarded couple ever to get married.

The answer, of course, is no. As far as can be ascertained, marriage between mildly retarded people occurs at about the same rate as marriage between members of any other so-called group—blacks, Jews, WASPs, or the nonretarded population in general.

In a follow-up study to his book *Cloak of Competence*, UCLA Professor Robert B. Edgerton came to the conclusion that it was hard to draw conclusions on the subject: There were some long-lasting marriages in the group of mildly retarded people he studied, some divorces, and some people who never married. Some retarded persons had good marriages, which were creative and satisfying; others saw marriage as a way to "pass" into the nonretarded community; it was their badge of normality. Others had marriages filled with poverty, depression, and sporadic violence. Edgerton's conclusion was that more work needed to be done.

Although Roger and Virginia had talked about marriage almost from the moment they met, the actuality of it had a galvanizing effect on their parents. Roger's sighed, bit their lips, and wondered what tensions this new adventure would bring. Virginia's family, living three hundred miles away, was upset.

Did Virginia need someone's permission to marry, since certain details from her parents' divorce were still unsettled after nearly seventeen years? Was this an experiment on the part of the residential facility and its counselors? Who were these counselors, and were they trained? Would the counseling continue after marriage? What part did sex play in their desire to marry? Had retarded persons been known to marry before? What about children? What about future legal entanglements the couple might get into? Who would be responsible for their debts and contracts? How much independence would Roger and Virginia be permitted to have? Would they lose their SSI money if they married?

These and other questions were put in a five-page letter written by Virginia's mother to Roger's parents on January 24, 1977. The questions shed light on the unique relationship that exists between the mildly retarded adult, who is able to function with help in the community, and his family, from whom he can still receive much assistance. The questions are those anyone might ask.

For example, although Roger and Virginia each knew that they could get married without their families' permission, each desperately wanted that permission—both because they wanted to be married with the glow of family blessings, and also because they knew they depended upon their families for advice, help, and love.

A pow-wow was arranged for February 3, 1977, and it was attended by Virginia's mother, Roger's parents, Roger and Virginia, Hank Newman and Bill Stein.

Let Bill Stein, the psychiatric social worker, describe one scene that took place before the meeting. "Roger was really worried about the meeting. He was afraid they wouldn't be 'allowed' to get married. I'd seen him that morning; then he disappeared. Suddenly, while we're all standing in the parking lot, ready to go inside to answer the questions, he comes running up, all out of breath. He takes something out of his pocket, see, and it's Virginia's wedding ring. I remember this as clear as anything. He was standing by one of the cars; he takes the ring out of the little box and he slips it on her finger. He wanted her to have it for the meeting."

As a sign, as a symbol, as a statement.

Thus attired, Virginia sailed in; everyone trailed inside in her wake for the meeting and for the answers to the questions troubling her family. Because accurate responses were wanted for Virginia's brother, who was unable to attend the meeting, our mother suggested a tape recorder be used to record what they talked about. One was soon found, and the meeting began.

Since guardianship had never been obtained for Virginia or her legal independence taken away, she had the same legal rights to marry as anyone else. Marriage would not change Roger and Virginia's standing in the eyes of the state and federal social-service systems (although they would receive slightly less SSI money as a couple than as two unmarried adults). Marriage among retarded persons was well documented, and the results varied from couple to couple, as with nonretarded adults. The counselors, such as Stein, were well trained and qualified (Stein holds a master's degree). The proposed marriage was not an experiment being pushed by the facility, but the end result of Virginia's and Roger's desire to fulfill their lives. The facility had no intention of publicizing or capitalizing on the marriage of its two former residents.

This issue became a sore point between the families after I showed up at the marriage site intending to be not only best man but reporter: Virginia's mother later said she felt "double-crossed" by my writing about the couple, when she had thought the statement that there would be no publicity was all-inclusive. I told her that at the time of their meeting I had not announced to my parents or anyone else my interest in writing about the couple, because I did not want to do anything that would interfere with the decision-making process.

As independent people, Roger and Virginia would be responsible for their own debts and liabilities, as is anyone else. If they needed additional help or advice, as they probably would, they might get it from their parents or from the counselors and agencies which were then supplying it to them.

At one point, Virginia looked up at her mother and asked, "How many more questions do you have to ask before I can get married?"

Not many. Virginia's mother took the information back home, and a few days later the stumbling block was removed: The wedding would be just fine, blessed and all, especially if it were held far enough down the road so that proper plans could be made. Easter Sunday was too soon; the June 18 date was chosen.

"And then," said Bill Stein, "we really had to get busy."

In May 1974, Roger and Virginia had begun taking sex-education courses at the facility where they lived. The course, being given for the first time, was taught by Don Simons.

"The idea of the classes was to provide retarded persons with knowledge about themselves and others. The retarded have the same sex drives as anyone else, and like anyone else, they make better decisions with as much information as possible."

The courses did more than give specifics on reproduction and contraception. "We tried to teach people to honor each other, to respect each other and themselves. If our goal is for the retarded to lead as normal a life as possible, then they must have as much information as possible to do that," he said. The classes also dealt with pregnancy, emotions, and child-rearing.

"Neither Roger nor Virginia is congenitally retarded, so any child they might have stands as good a chance of being born nonretarded as does yours or mine. In our classes we talk about that, about the responsibility of rearing children, and whether that might be too much of a problem for some people. For too long, the retarded at all levels have been denied the chance to participate in their own lives," he said.

Simons had started the sex-education classes in anticipation of the construction of the Transitional Living Project apartments the following year. Since Roger and Virginia would be among the first to move into them, the sex-education courses were seen as logical preparation to the semi-independent life they would be leading.

The idea is far more progressive than it may seem. One recent court case dealt with the question of whether a judge who ordered the sterilization of a fifteen-year-old retarded girl in Indiana was judicially immune from liability under the federal civil rights statutes. The girl, who had attended school, was told the purpose of a hospital visit was an appendectomy. The girl later married, and two years after, in 1975, discovered she had been sterilized without her knowledge or consent. The suit claimed, among other things, that her constitutional rights had been violated.

The girl's mother had requested that the judge order the sterilization, which he did. But the girl was not represented by counsel or informed of what was happening.

Had her constitutional rights been violated? A bitterly divided U.S. Supreme Court, in March, 1978, ruled that judges have absolute immunity and cannot be sued for damages, regardless of the orders they issue.

That girl had been living at home. But it has also been common practice in institutions for retarded adults to be sterilized without their knowledge, or to be sterilized as an informal condition of their release. Additionally, some people in the field say that, currently, birth-control pills are put in the water or coffee of retarded women—a less drastic form of birth control, but still one that is involuntary.

With this traditional approach to the subject as a background, the idea of garden-variety sex-education classes for the retarded may really seem radical.

As they approached their own wedding, Roger and Virginia knew about sex, about intercourse, about orgasms, about pregnancy, and about everything else that people in their twenties know about. They had declined to participate in a full range of intimacy because they felt that was most properly done within the context of marriage. But within that context of marriage, they also wanted, very badly, to have children.

"That's what regular people do," Roger said. "They get married and have children and have a house. That's what we wanted, too."

Roger and Virginia believed it was virtually the moral obligation of married couples to have children, and they held this belief until only several months before their wedding. Roger occasionally talks about it now. But their parents did not share this feeling, at least where the two of them were concerned.

"We really were worried about what would happen if there were kids," our mother said. "We honestly didn't believe they could handle the situation." Virginia's mother echoed this feeling.

Our parents talked with Richard Koch, M.D., at Children's Hospital, in Los Angeles, and learned from him of studies which showed that the retardation of a mother is a more important factor in a child's development or lack of it than the retardation of the father. At the same time, they learned Koch's feeling that retarded people should not have children because they are unable to provide the child with a stimulating enough atmosphere to promote normal intellectual growth. "This also starts the cycle of environmentally-caused retardation, poor self-image, poverty, and so on," he told them.

In almost every conversation their parents had with them, the "don't have kids" line was given to Virginia and Roger. There was the strongly-implied idea that their parents' "blessings" for the marriage might be withdrawn unless some assurances were given that they would not have children. Nevertheless, the couple did not surrender their beliefs.

"They were getting such pressure from their parents not to have children that they started looking for any way out they could find," Bill Stein said. "One day they said they had seen a television show the night before, in which some children had been brutally murdered. They said that they were afraid that if they had kids, the same fate might happen to them. I rejected that line; I just would not accept it. I told them, if that were true, then nobody should have children, including me—and they had met my kids. It was really rough on them."

For years Virginia had been saying, "What if we had kids and they weren't retarded and they came home from school and asked us something we couldn't answer? What would they think of us then?" (This is really the situation that can cause environmentally-induced retardation.) But under prodding from Roger, she always backed off this view, at least in his company. Kids for him were the final badge of normality, the final proof that he had overcome his retardation, and he would not surrender that belief without a fight.

"Once during a telephone call he told us that he had decided not to have kids," our mother remembers. "He said he had decided to have only one kid."

"Your parents," Stein sighed. "Every time I heard from them they were worried about this business about kids. I said, 'Look, I'm trying to get them to cross the street safely. We'll handle the question of kids as soon as we can.'"

Stein's blunt-talking ways, couched in a fragrant New York accent, were extraordinarily reassuring to them. Our parents came to rely on Stein for guidance, as they relied on no other person. They called him at home, they called him at work, and at times he ended up counseling them as much as he was counseling Roger and Virginia. His attitude was: "It's great they're interested, coming to see Roger all the time, that helps Roger's growth enormously." But he kept telling them they had to let go. For our parents' part they framed a snapshot of Stein and some other counselors and put it on a bedside table, almost turning the Bronx-born counselor into a third son.

One day, Stein drove Roger and Virginia to their local regional center for genetic testing. Roger was specifically being tested for Tay-Sachs disease, an inherited error of metabolism which appears mainly in people of Middle European Jewish ancestry. The test is conducted by the painful insertion of needles to withdraw blood samples.

"Roger took the test, and then Virginia said she wanted to

take it, too," Barbara Dixson, the genetic counselor who worked with them at the regional center, recalled. "I told her she didn't have to, because she was not from the same background as Roger's family, so she couldn't possibly be a carrier. But she said that since Roger had undergone the tests, she wanted to undergo the tests."

Dixson inserted the needles, searching for the right vein.

"Virginia's veins are so small it took several attempts until one was found," said Stein, who was there. "It was painful as anything, but she never showed it."

"Even though Virginia has scoliosis (or curvature of the spine), she could have probably carried a child without much problem," Dixson said. "It would have been so easy if there had been a genetic or physical reason why they could not have children. It would have been so easy if the decision had been handed to them. But it wasn't. They had to make up their own minds."

"Roger thought of children as wonderful little toys, as objects to play with. I don't think he fully realized all the responsibility involved," Stein said. "Once I asked him what he would do if a baby woke up at three o'clock in the morning for a feeding, and he said he'd call a babysitter. Finally, I think Virginia became concerned that a child, however wonderful, might really be a disruptive force in their lives, might hurt their marriage. I think when she made up her mind, that was it."

Then, like millions of other couples around the world, they took proper steps to avoid conception during their upcoming marriage.

"It was one of the toughest decisions of their lives," Stein said.

Their counseling with Stein, sometimes once a week, sometimes more, was voluntary on their part. It was a sign of how much they wanted to learn about this brave new world of independence. In their counseling, they talked about Roger's temper, Virginia's tendency to mother him, the problems they had in dealing with their parents, marriage, having children, and jobs.

Virginia said she would like to participate in a job-training program that would lead to hotel work, but only after the wedding. Right now, she was under too much stress. Stein said that sounded like a good idea.

Roger had his restaurant job, from which he derived esteem, self-satisfaction, and money. He told Stein that "It would be better for us if Virginia works after we're married." What about his own employment? After all, he only worked twenty hours a week, if that. He was surely capable of handling a full-time job.

"Well, I want to be a teacher. I was very popular with the children at the home. I could help them with things, like I helped Lionel with his handwriting," Roger said.

Stein listened to this belief of Roger's, and one day said, "Roger, you don't even have a high school diploma. You have a special education equivalency certificate. To be a teacher you need a college degree."

Roger responded, "It took me twenty years to learn how to do long division. In another twenty years I could learn how to do the things I don't know about now."

Stein questioned this: "There are so many things in college, advanced mathematics, English literature, science, and social studies. With mental retardation, learning comes slowly, and sometimes you can't get beyond a certain point."

Roger argued that he had taught himself how to carry numbers, and that with time he could learn how to do geometry.

He also said that he had enrolled in a woodworking class during the evening adult sessions at a local high school, and that way he would train himself to be a toymaker. He said that when he took long bus rides he became "frustrated and tired," so he wouldn't want to travel too far if he got a toymaker's job. Periodically, he would come back to his desire to be a teacher, principally because of the adulation of younger people. Whenever the subject of Roger being a teacher came up, Stein pointed up the realities.

To show both Roger and Virginia that mental retardation was not an all-encompassing lock on them, Stein one day devised an extraordinary exercise.

He had Roger and Virginia each go into a separate room,

close the door, shut their eyes, and take all their clothes off. The idea was to get dressed again in as perfect a fashion as possible.

"I wanted them to see that they did not have to rely only on their eyes to get dressed, that they could use other faculties— memory, touch. I wanted them to fully appreciate that just because they were handicapped in some areas, they were not handicapped in others, and they could use their good faculties to make up for the others."

Roger plotted his course fairly well, coming out of his room earlier than Virginia, who had some trouble with the organization of the sequence of her clothing without using her eyes.

"But, when she came out, she said she had never realized the problems blind people had. She has a friend who is blind, and she said she never before realized the difficulties her friend has," Stein said.

Time had flown quickly, and their counseling sessions were almost over. Stein was about to leave his job and move to northern California with his family. At their last session together, he, Roger, and Virginia talked about the coming marriage, about what they had learned, and about what they would work on with Carol Knieff, who was their new counselor.

At the end of their time together, Stein hunched over in his chair, his voice very low, hands clasped between his knees.

"I thanked them for letting me work with them," he said. "I told them how much I had learned from them—about how they communicated with each other with their words, and bodies, and emotions. I told them that they had taught me how to look at myself and be honest with myself, as they were struggling to do with themselves. They had taught me how to encounter someone else and be honest with him, be honest with yourself; not ignore or prejudge someone just because he is different. They respected each other's right to be different, and I appreciated that. We helped each other in those counseling sessions," Bill Stein said. "All I did was listen."

Shortly afterward, on May 24, 1977, as he was preparing to move to his new home, Stein wrote our parents a letter:

Dear Bob & Roz,

By far this is the most difficult good-by I will have to make to any family I have known the past five years.

I've once heard it said that happiness is not a station you arrive at but the way you travel—I hope [my new home town] will not be my station, just a way of traveling—

We have traveled, too—a long way together. Roger was the conductor and we were the passengers—and that we must never forget—For it is often the other way around. He was indeed a good leader, for he brought us together to work with him and not for him. He made us realize our responsibilities not just as family and social worker but as people who can listen, who can learn, who can change, and most of all, who can care.

For every stage that Roger journeyed, so did we—sometimes with pain, often with fear, but always with love—I thank him for that.

I stated in my letter of resignation that I will deeply miss working in the field of Developmental Disabilities—well, it is not the field that I will miss, but all the Rogers and his families and friends that have helped me grow—and that is where my rewards are.

So when I say good-by to you now I will not be leaving, but rather just taking you and your family with me in my travels.

My love,

[signed] Bill

The day before the wedding, Stein boarded a bus and traveled 330 miles all day long through the hot and dusty central valley of California to be a witness to his friends' wedding.

"Why me? Why did this have to happen to me?" our father said to me, shortly before the wedding. "Why us? Had we done something? Were we being punished for something? I used to ask myself those questions all the time, but never got an answer. Because the answer really is, Why *not* me? What's so special about me? About us? Nothing really; we're ordinary people. So this is something we've lived with, and who can say how our lives would have been different if Roger had not been retarded. But I can tell you this: Roger would have reached his potential a lot earlier if the programs that are available now had been available when he was growing up."

The wedding was scheduled for 1:30 in the afternoon. At 12:45, back at the hotel, our father decided he had to have a sandwich, and then a cup of coffee, and then another cup.

Our mother, who was dressed and ready to go, begged him to leave. But our father, sixty-seven years old and having seen a side of life different from what he'd expected when his youngest son was born twenty-eight years previously, continued to sit in the hotel coffee shop, stirring his coffee, and watching the steam slowly rise and disappear, curl upward to the ceiling and slowly vanish. He was lost in thought and memory as the minutes ticked away, a lifetime passing before him. The ceremony was delayed for ten minutes until our parents took their place in the front pew.

 **17**

STANDING STRONG

Here I stand, with open hands
Reaching out for other lands.
Working hard night and day,
Helping people all the way.
Standing strong, and doing nothing
That is wrong. Looking for the
Beauty bright, doing all things that are right.

—ROGER MEYERS

On December 9, 1977, Beatrice Houghtellin slipped and fell in her apartment, smashing her head against the kitchen stove, breaking her nose, and losing consciousness. When she regained it, she was on the floor, unable to get up. She was a woman of seventy-six whose legs "frequently go out from under me."

The telephone was too far away to be of use: She couldn't even drag herself there. Although she cried out for help, no one answered. It is unclear from her own recollection how long she stayed on the floor. She thinks it was no more than two hours, although from other details it may have been as much as six hours.

At 11:45 P.M. that night, Roger Meyers was arriving home from work. Mrs. Houghtellin's apartment is next to Roger's and Virginia's. He heard her calling out for help, and opened her door, which; because she has fallen frequently in the past, she often leaves unlocked.

"When I saw her I said, 'Oh, my God! I'll call an ambulance.' Her face was burned."

Roger then went to his apartment and dialed the operator. "I said there was a neighbor who was hurt, and I wanted the number of the police. So she gave it to me. Then I called the police and told them her name, address, apartment number, and said they should send an ambulance. They asked me my name and address and telephone number, too. I told them."

A few minutes later, a rescue ambulance and three police squad cars, with lights flashing, arrived at the scene. Mrs. Houghtellin was taken to the hospital, where she was treated and released the next day.

"There is absolutely no question in my mind that a year ago Roger would not have done that," said Anita Tracy, the manager of the apartment building, who was awakened by the commotion. "If she had asked him to call the police, he would have come looking for me or my husband to ask us what he should do. If he couldn't have found us, I really think he would have waited for morning. With a woman that age, you never know what a wait like that could mean. It's very possible he saved her life."

As a reward, Mrs. Houghtellin gave Roger five dollars. "She told me to buy cranberry juice with it, because she knows that's what I like," he said.

When he showed the five-dollar bill to Mrs. Tracy, she said, "He held it out as if it were a thousand."

The growth and maturity of Roger and Virginia Meyers since their June 18, 1977, wedding has been phenomenal. Their calmness, seriousness, and sense of self are just stunning. The incident involving Mrs. Houghtellin is remarkable, precisely because it is such an unremarkable event: A neighbor needed help, and a young man called the police. It is the kind of responsible act that people do every day, but of which the retarded are thought incapable. Maybe they are, when they are given no real-life experience and when the expectations of their abilities are kept so low. So, maybe, it is time to revise upward our expectations of retarded citizens.

Several weeks later, two women from the Jehovah's Witnesses religion knocked on his door. Roger talked with them a while, and said he would buy an inexpensive Bible when they came back to see him, as they said they would. Three days later they did. "I said they could come in. One sat in the big chair, and another sat on the couch with me. I told them more about my religion, about Christian Science and the *Key to the Scriptures* by Mary Baker Eddy. Then they started telling me that was wrong. They said Jehovah came first, before anything, but I said that wasn't until the second book of Genesis, that what came first was the first book of Genesis, and there the spiritual man created in the image and likeness of God was created. They kept arguing with me, and I got mad. They showed me the Bible they wanted me to buy, but I saw it wasn't the King James version. It was different. So I said to give me my money back, and they did.

"They kept arguing with me and, finally, I said I didn't want them to be here anymore. I got mad and I yelled at them to get out; then I opened the door and told them to leave. They did."

Anita Tracy, the apartment manager, was walking nearby and heard a ruckus she thought meant the end of the world had come. But it was only Roger, standing up for his rights.

After the wedding, I returned to Washington and spent three weeks writing the series, which ran in the Washington *Post* on August 21, 22, and 23, 1977. The response was quite large. Letters and telephone calls came in from people with similar success stories to tell, along with stories of frustrations and heartaches of those that had not worked out as well.

One woman wrote to tell of her retarded brother, whose brain damage had led him to self-destructive acts against himself and others. Given absolutely no help or treatment, he had finally beaten his head against a wall so often that he died of self-inflicted wounds. She wrote that Roger's and Virginia's success "vindicated" her late brother.

One man told about the professional gardening work his son had; a woman wrote about the progress her daughter was making in her marriage.

Other people wrote to say that because the real names of the people involved had been used, they were now encouraged to talk about their own experiences. Because the *Post* had given front-page display to a real-life story, they felt they no longer had to hide their own knowledge.

Among the letters I liked best were those from people who said they had no connection with mental retardation in their families at all, but that because of Roger's and Virginia's successes, their minds had been opened as to what retardation was, and what could be done about it.

However, there were many calls and letters that showed that the vast array of attitudinal changes, research, training techniques, and knowledge about federal, state, and local assistance had not yet filtered down to the general public. Many people asked for help and information, wanting to know whom they could contact in their area. It is remarkable that for all that has been done, so much more can be done.

Virginia wrote thank-you notes for the wedding gifts, and Roger kept on with his restaurant job. Not surprisingly in a world in which they were being encouraged to live as much as possible within the normal rhythm of life, the first trouble spots in their marriage came from their in-laws.

"They were getting," Carol Knieff said diplomatically, "a great deal of input from both sides." Not too different from what most marriages are like, but they were very disturbing to these newlyweds who have to fight for every step of their lives.

"We went to a marriage counselor," Roger said, mentioning a psychiatrist with experience in dealing with the retarded. "He gave us tips on what to do."

These tips, which he is not willing to give away, worked. The in-law problems calmed down, as did the in-laws; after all, the marriage of these particular children was something none of them had ever really expected, and they had a lot of adjusting to do, too.

Virginia began training as a hotel employee, spending three hours each day doing on-the-job work. When she finishes, she will earn the minimum wage for competitive employment.

"We decided we needed more experience in doing things for ourselves," Virginia told me recently. "So in honor of George Washington's birthday we spent a night in a hotel, making the reservation and paying for it ourselves. It cost us six dollars, at the place where I work. My boss picked up half the bill, six dollars and seventy-two cents. We had dinner that night at

Bob's Big Boy, and we said it was as if you or your dad was feeding us. Then we had breakfast at the International House of Pancakes—the breakfast special with pancakes, hash browns, and two eggs any way you like them. But don't worry, honey, Roger's not gaining any weight at all. He really looks terrific."

Roger decided he would like to earn more money, at the same time as he tried to compensate for not having children in his marriage. So with Virginia's agreement, he placed a classified ad in the local newspaper, offering "experienced babysitters, for children three to ten, our apartment, across from schoolyard."

Although there were several telephone inquiries, there were no clients. Roger's parents, however, hit the roof when he told them about the scheme.

"What if someone had gone to their apartment and robbed them? What if a baby got sick and they did not recognize it?" our father railed. "Where were the counselors on this?"

The counselors, of course, were just as much in the dark about the newlyweds' plans as anyone else, which is what happens when independent people take independent action. The normalization principle was now on the other foot, and it pinched.

Once everyone calmed down, however, Roger learned—much to his displeasure—that the standard rental contract he and Virginia had did not allow businesses to be conducted in the apartment. Also, that in order to take children into his own home for babysitting purposes, he had to have a license from the county.

He now occasionally talks about full-time work as a busboy, dishwasher, or janitorial aide, or working as an aide in a child care center.

He continues to talk about a job as a teacher. It appears that he hates the designation "mentally retarded" so much he would rather work twenty years in the hopes of getting a teaching job, a position held by the nonretarded, than get a full-time job now, if he still has the hated label on him.

His courageous desire to rid himself of that label, however, also drains him of the energy needed to make himself more independent.

Are Roger and Virginia still retarded? Under the standard definition of mental retardation developed by the American Association on Mental Deficiency in 1973, a retarded person is one whose I.Q. is about 70, one who has adaptive behavior problems, and one whose situation is observed during the developmental stage of life, usually up to about age eighteen.

Roger and Virginia are both adults, they are married, and are jobholders. Some recent I.Q. tests have placed their latest scores slightly over that level. More important, however, they are learning to work around their disabilities.

In *Mental Retardation: Past and Present*, published by the President's Committee on Mental Retardation, is this statement: "Who are the people who are mentally retarded? They are individuals whose assets for effective living in their cultural and physical environments are insufficient without assistance."

From behavioral psychologist Marc Gold, Ph.D., comes this alternative definition: "Mental retardation refers to a level of functioning which requires from society above-average training procedures and superior assets in adaptive behavior, manifested throughout life."

Roger Meyers has said, "People are retarded by what they don't know. That's why I work so hard to learn the things I don't know and to become more normal."

These definitions capture the humanistic spirit of the work that has been going on in the field: The medical model, with its concept of incurable illness, is being replaced by the developmental model, in which some people are seen to need certain kinds of help over a longer than usual period of time.

Can mental retardation be cured? No one has said it can be, although its impact can be lessened in such a way that the individual no longer functions within the defined range of mental retardation. With at least 250 individual causes of mental retardation identified, it is almost certain that no one "magic bullet" cure will be found. The leading consumer group, the National Association for Retarded Citizens, recently set out a five-year plan to "identify cures for disorders and conditions involved in mental retardation. . . ."

What if Roger and Virginia were born today? Would their stories be any different if they were written thirty years from now, in the year 2008, rather than 1978? As some of the responses to The Washington *Post* series indicated, many people today do not know anything about the available sources of help. They do not know what mental retardation is, how its impact can be lessened, or how its stress can be blunted. So, quite possibly, the story of Roger and Virginia could be repeated in coming decades—though not necessarily.

One of the great thrusts in the field is in the area of prevention: vast amounts of material are available in simple, understandable form. The medical profession has become much more enlightened as to retardation, and what can be done to avoid its occurrence or lessen its impact. The cavalier order to warehouse a retarded baby is no longer given by all physicians, although it is still given by some.

Early intervention is an important concept, in which trained social workers show a mother how to raise a retarded child, how to make him suck, swallow, chew, and respond. All help is provided at comparatively low cost to society and to its great eventual benefit.

Early education is often available in which a child's brain and physical capabilities are exercised to their fullest, for the maximum advantage.

The stigma of having a retarded child is lessening, although it is still strong and often unconsciously expressed by well-meaning people. (A relative recently referred to Roger's retardation as "tragic," the kind of phrase which makes the speaker feel good about not doing anything to alleviate the situation.)

The continued integration of the retarded into normal society, and the education of the retarded alongside their nonretarded classmates now are concepts fixed in law; both groups will probably benefit.

In Denmark, the mental retardation services branch headed by N. E. Bank-Mikkelsen will be absorbed by an overall social services department in 1980. Bank-Mikkelsen says that this is the natural consequence of the normalization principle, so that retarded persons will soon be regarded in the same light as any other person in need of services. In this country, a proposal has been made to abolish the President's Committee on Mental

Retardation and move its functions under a more general Developmental Disabilities umbrella. People in the field here feel that they would lose the status and clout they have worked so hard to get and be relegated once more to the bottom of the human-services totem pole. The issue is now being debated in Washington.

For my brother and sister-in-law, if their SSI funds and services cease (which will happen when their earned income goes over $200 per month for each of them), they will have no more or less social services available to them than would any other couple, though they may need them. If one of them becomes unemployed, they will have access to their state unemployment insurance, and, if necessary, their state's welfare system. According to Carol Knieff, the managers of the SSI program at the moment do not feel that someone who gets off SSI should ever be taken back onto it.

Roger and Virginia may need help, however, even when they are both fully employed. They may need guidance; they may need counseling. In the absence of public aid, or their ability to pay for private services or get help from their families, they might be able to find some kind of citizen advocate who could help them.

This is a comparatively new concept, which basically relies on unpaid volunteers who serve as "friends" or "guides" or "helpers" for retarded persons. Sometimes the advocates have specific duties—I have met several in northern Virginia who are "apartment advocates," helping their retarded friends to find apartments and to live successfully in them. Others serve a more general role; helping their friends on a situation-by-situation basis.

Roger and Virginia's story is unique only because it has been told. There are many similar stories which are equally as complex, equally as moving, but which have not yet been written down. In the future they will be, and more people can discover, as Bill Stein did, how much they can learn from the Rogers and Virginias of this world.

In mid-October First Lady Rosalynn Carter began researching material for the keynote address she would make on November 4 in New Orleans to the annual convention of the National Association for Retarded Citizens. She felt that the *Post* series on the young couple might be incorporated into her speech. A White House aide called the paper and asked if Mrs. Carter could meet with the reporter.

We met in her sunny office, its walls painted yellow. She motioned me to sit next to her on a couch, while her aides sat nearby, taking notes. I found out what it was like to be interviewed.

She said that when she had read the series in August, it had reminded her of an incident in 1953, when she and her husband, who then had just gotten out of the Navy, moved into a hundred-year-old farmhouse.

"One of our boys found a secret room in the attic; he found it by removing some bricks from a chimney. In the room was a little chair," she said.

Inquiries with neighbors yielded nothing definitive, but the story that kept surfacing over and over again was that the room had been used to hide someone the family did not want to be seen—quite possibly a mentally retarded relative.

"That made a deep impression on me; it has always stayed with me," Mrs. Carter said. "The contrast between the existence of that secret compartment and the way in which your parents treated Roger was vivid in my mind," she said.

We talked about the development of the parents' movement, about the current knowledge in the field, and the availability of federal, state, and local funds—but also about the fact that many people still did not know where to go for help and still did not know that mental retardation is a fact of life, not the end of the world. Most of all, we talked about the change in attitude, about the slow and sometimes grudging recognition of the rights of retarded people, and about the fact that people who are retarded are people, no more, no less.

Mrs. Carter made her speech in the main ballroom of the Fairmont Hotel in New Orleans before 2,700 NARC members. She wove Roger's and Virginia's story throughout her address, and afterward introduced me to the audience. Several weeks later I sent my parents a commercially-produced tape of the speech. When he played it, alone in his study, my father broke down and cried.

I spoke with my brother the other day to check some facts. Again and again and again, I wonder with pride at the maturity he is showing. Our conversations are longer than they have been before. He can sustain interest and comment on a single topic for longer than ever before; his voice is deeper. Having once identified only with people who themselves were treated only as children. Roger is more and more seeing himself as an adult, a person of dignity and purpose. I am now thinking of taking a vacation with my brother and his wife. *With my brother*!

Our parents spent Christmas Day at Roger and Virginia's apartment. It had really not been too many months before that Roz Meyers could not do such a thing. She could not spend all that much time with her younger son, because of the pains that came over her—the memories and fears returned and the tension, literally, forced her to sit down. But times change, and so do people who are struggling to make themselves whole.

Christmas Day, the two women were in the kitchen, wearing aprons, and exchanging recipes for turkeys and dressing. They would eat when Roger got home from work. Our father was in the living room, watching TV, ready to carve the turkey when the time came.

Virginia's mother had called; I soon phoned. The families had made contact.

When our mother felt a bit tired, she went into the bedroom to rest. Before napping, she took a small notepad and pencil out of her purse, and jotted down some of the things that had been said that day, some of the things that had been done, some of her thoughts and feelings. These she sent to Washington, to her other son, the one who writes.

One of the Christmas cards Roger and Virginia received came in a beige envelope with a Washington, D.C., postmark. The front of the card featured a large six-columned house with a flag on top. Inside was the message: "With best wishes from our family for a Merry Christmas and a Happy New Year." The printed signature showed the card was from "The President and Mrs. Carter." Several days later a thank-you note bearing a California postmark was mailed to the White House. Inside the message read: "Thank you very much for your Christmas card, and best wishes for the New Year." The signature showed the card was from Virginia and Roger Meyers.

"How is it with us?" Virginia Meyers asked, a woman who, like her husband and millions of people like them, has pulled herself up by her own bootstraps to achieve her full humanity. "It's no different than it is with anyone else, except that we're slower."

Appendix

The National Association for Retarded Citizens (NARC) is the largest organization of parents and friends of retarded persons in this country. There are more than 1,900 local chapters spread throughout the United States. What follows is a list containing the address of NARC's national headquarters, and then the locations of the headquarters for each of the fifty states and for the District of Columbia. The state headquarters can provide the location of a nearby chapter.

National Association for Retarded Citizens
2709 Avenue E East
P.O. Box 6109
Arlington, Texas 76011

STATE ASSOCIATIONS FOR RETARDED CITIZENS

ALABAMA: 4301 Normal Road, Montgomery, AL 36105—(205) 288-9434

ALASKA: SR Box 30188, Fairbanks, AK 99701—(907) 479-4098-H

ARIZONA: 5610 S. Central, Phoenix, AZ 85040—(602) 268-2200

ARKANSAS: Fausett Plaza, Suite 410, University at Markham, Little Rock, AR 72205—(501) 661-1220

CALIFORNIA: 1225 Eight Street, Suite 312, Sacramento, CA 95814—(916) 441-3322

COLORADO: 2727 Bryant Street L-3, Denver, CO 80211—(303) 455-4411

CONNECTICUT: 15 High Street, Hartford, CT 06103—(203) 522-1179 or 657-2680-H

DELAWARE: P.O. Box 1896, Wilmington, DE 19899—(302) 764-3662-B

WASHINGTON, D.C.: 405 Riggs Road, N.E., Washington, DC 20011—(202) 529-0070

FLORIDA: P.O. Box 1542, Tallahassee, FL 32302—(904) 878-6121

GEORGIA: 1575 Phoenix Boulevard, Suite 8, Atlanta, GA 30349—(404) 996-4116

HAWAII: 245 N. Kukui Street, Honolulu, HI 96817—(808) 536-2274

IDAHO: P.O. Box 816, Boise, ID 83701—(208) B-345-8190

ILLINOIS: #6 North Michigan Avenue, Chicago, IL 60602—(312) 263-7135

INDIANA: 752 E. Market Street, Indianapolis, IN 46202—(317) 632-4387 or 784-7157

IOWA: 1707 High Street, Des Moines, IA 50309—(515) 283-2358

KANSAS: 6100 Martway, Suite #1, Mission, KA 66202—(913)236-6810

KENTUCKY: P.O. Box 275, Frankfort, KY 40601—(502) 564-7050

LOUISIANA: 2119 Wooddale Boulevard, Baton Rouge, LA 70806—(504) 927-4064

MAINE: P.O. Box 2267, Augusta, ME 04330—(207) 622-7161

MARYLAND: 55 Gwynns Mill Court, Owings Mills, MD 21117—(301) 356-3410

MASSACHUSETTS: 318 Elliot Street, Newton Upper Falls, MA 20164—(617) 965-5320

MICHIGAN: 416 Michigan National Tower Building, Lansing, MI 48933—(517) 487-5426

MINNESOTA: 3225 Lyndale Avenue, S., Minneapolis, MN 55408—(612) 827-5641

MISSISSIPPI: 3000 Old Canton Road, P.O. Box 1363, Jackson, MS 39205—(601) 362-7981

MISSOURI: 230 W. Dunklin, Jefferson City, MO 65101—(314) 634-2220

MONTANA: 27 Grand Avenue, Billings, MT 59101—(406) 587-8546

NEBRASKA: 3100 N. 14th, Lower Level, Lincoln, NB 68521—(402) 467-4408

NEVADA: 1450 E. Second Street, Reno, NV 89502—(702) 322-7255

NEW HAMPSHIRE: 110 N. Main Street, Concord, NH 03301—(603) 224-7322

NEW JERSEY: 99 Bayard Street, New Brunswick, NJ 08901—(201) 246-2525

NEW MEXICO: $8200^{1}/_{2}$ Menaul Boulevard, N.E., Suite #3, Albuquerque, NM 87110—(505) 298-6796

NEW YORK: 254 West 31 Street, Suite 304, New York, NY 10001—(212) 689-9290

NORTH CAROLINA: P.O. Box 18551, Raleigh, NC 27609—(919) 782-5114-B

NORTH DAKOTA: 1223 South 12 Street, Bismarck, NC 58501—(701) 223-5349

OHIO: 8 E. Long Street, 9th Floor, Columbus, OH 43215—(614) 228-6689

OKLAHOMA: P.O. Box 14250, Oklahoma City, OK 73114—(405) 842-8834 or H-848-4520

OREGON: 3085 River Road, N., Salem, OR 97303—(503) 588-0095

PENNSYLVANIA: 1500 N. Second, Harrisburg, PA 17102—(717) B-234-2621

RHODE ISLAND: 2845 Post Road, Warwick, RI 20886—(401) 738-5550

SOUTH CAROLINA: P.O. Box 1564, Columbia, SC 29202—(803) 765-2431

SOUTH DAKOTA: P.O. Box 502, 111 W. Capitol, Pierre, SD 57501—(605) 224-8211

TENNESSEE: 1700 Hayes Street, Suite 201, Nashville, TN 37203—(615) 327-0294

TEXAS: 833 W. Houston, Austin, TX 78756—(512) 454-6694

UTAH: 1588 South Major Street, Salt Lake City, UT 84115—(801) 486-0773

VERMONT: 323 Pearl Street, Burlington, VA 05401—(802) 864-0761

VIRGINIA: 827 E. Main Street, Suite 1801, Richmond, VA 22030—(703) 273-6226

WASHINGTON: 805 Williams Boulevard, Richland, WA 99352—(509) B-946-7114

WEST VIRGINIA: Union Trust Bldg. Room 514, Parkersburg, WV 26101—(304) 485-5283

WISCONSIN: 2700 Laura Lane, Middleton, WI 53562—(608) 831-3444 or 238-2190-H

WYOMING: Box 1205, Cheyenne, WY 82001—(307) 632-7105-B or 634-9545-H

The following is a list of some other national organizations dealing with mental retardation and other developmental disabilities.

American Association on Mental Deficiency
5201 Connecticut Avenue, N.W.
Washington, DC 20015

American Civil Liberties Union
85 Fifth Avenue
New York, NY 10011

Center for Law and Social Policy
1600 Twentieth St., N.W.
Washington, DC 20005

Center on Human Policy
216 Ostrom Avenue
Syracuse, NY 13210

Council for Exceptional Children
1920 Association Drive
Reston, VA 22091

Mental Health Law Project
84 Fifth Avenue
New York, NY 10011

or

1751 N. Street, N.W.
Washington, DC 20036

National Chapter for Law and the Handicapped
1235 N. Eddy Street
South Bend, IN 46617

President's Committee on Employment
   of the Handicapped
1111 Twentieth St., N.W.
Washington, DC 20210

President's Committee on Mental Retardation
Washington, DC 20201

Selected Bibliography

American Medical Association. *Mental Retardation*. Chicago: American Medical Association, 1974.

Blatt, Burtan, and Fred Kaplan. *Christmas in Purgatory: A Photographic Essay on Mental Retardation*. Syracuse, NY: Human Policy Press, 1974.

de la Cruz, F., and Gerald D. LaVeck, eds. *Human Sexuality and the Mentally Retarded*. New York: Brunner/Mazek, 1973.

Edgerton, Robert B. *The Cloak of Competence*. Berkeley and Los Angeles: University of California Press, 1967.

Friedman, Paul R. *The Rights of Mentally Retarded Persons: An American Civil Liberties Handbook*. New York: Discus/Avon, 1976.

Itard, Jean-Marc-Gaspard. *The Wild Boy of Aveyron*. Englewood Cliffs, NJ: Prentice-Hall, 1962.

Koch, Richard and Kathryn Jean Koch. *Understanding the Mentally Retarded Child: A New Approach*. New York: Random House, 1974.

Menolascino, Frank J., ed. *Psychiatric Approaches to Mental Retardation*. New York: Basic Books, 1970.

President's Committee on Mental Retardation. *Changing Patterns in Residential Services for the Mentally Retarded*, edited by Robert B. Kugel and Wolf Wolfensberger. Washington, DC: President's Committee on Mental Retardation, 1969.

_____. *Mental Retardation: Century of Decision*. Washington, DC: President's Committee on Mental Retardation, 1976.

_____. *Mental Retardation: The Known and the Unknown*. Washington, DC: President's Committee on Mental Retardation, 1975.

_____. *Mental Retardation: Past and Present*. Washington, DC: President's Committee on Mental Retardation, 1977.

_____. *Mental Retardation: Trends in State Services*. Washington, DC: President's Committee on Mental Retardation, 1976.

_____. *New Neighbors: The Retarded Citizen in Quest of a Home*. Washington, DC: President's Committee on Mental Retardation, 1974.

_____. *The Six-Hour Retarded Child*. Washington, DC: President's Committee on Mental Retardation, 1969.

Wolfensberger, Wolf. *The Origin and Nature of our Institutional Models*. Syracuse, NY: Human Policy Press, 1975

Wolfensberger, Wolf and Bengt Nirje, Simon Olshansky, Robert Perske, Philip Roos. *The Principle of Normalization in Human Services*. Toronto: National Institute on Mental Retardation, 1972.

Wolfensberger, Wolf and Helen Zauha, eds. *Citizen Advocacy and Protective Services for the Impaired and Handicapped*. Toronto: National Institute on Mental Retardation, 1973.